Leadership Essentials

SHAPING VISION, MULTIPLYING INFLUENCE, DEFINING CHARACTER

Greg Ogden *and* Daniel Meyer

IVP Connect

An imprint of InterVarsity Press
Downers Grove, Illinois

InterVarsity Press
P.O. Box 1400, Downers Grove, IL 60515-1426
World Wide Web: www.ivpress.com
E-mail: email@ivpress.com

InterVarsity Press® is the book-publishing division of InterVarsity Christian Fellowship/USA®, a student movement active on campus at hundreds of universities, colleges and schools of nursing in the United States of America, and a member movement of the International Fellowship of Evangelical Students. For information about local and regional activities, write Public Relations Dept., InterVarsity Christian Fellowship/USA, 6400 Schroeder Rd., P.O. Box 7895, Madison, WI 53707-7895, or visit the IVCF website at <www.intervarsity.org>.

All Scripture quotations, unless otherwise indicated, are taken from the Holy Bible, New International Version® NIV®. Copyright ©1973, 1978, 1984 by International Bible Society. Used by permission of Zondervan Publishing House. All rights reserved.

Design: Cindy Kiple
Images: Gary S. Chapman/Getty Images

ISBN 978-0-8308-1097-0

Printed in the United States of America ∞

Library of Congress Cataloging-in-Publication Data

Ogden, Greg.
 Leadership essentials: shaping vision, multiplying influence,
 defining character / Greg Ogden and Dan Meyer.
  p. cm
 Includes bibliographical references.
 ISBN-13: 978-0-8308-1097-0 (pbk.: alk. paper)
 1. Leadership—Religious aspects—Christianity. I. Meyer, Dan,
 1959- II. Title.
 BV4597.53.L43O33 2007
 248.4017—dc22

2007031450

| P | 24 | 23 | 22 | 21 | 20 | 19 | 18 | 17 | 16 | 15 | 14 | 13 | 12 | 11 | 10 | 9 | 8 | 7 | 6 | 5 | 4 | 3 | 2 | 1 |
| Y | 28 | 27 | 26 | 25 | 24 | 23 | 22 | 21 | 20 | 19 | 18 | 17 | 16 | 15 | 14 | 13 | 12 | 11 | 10 | 09 | 08 | 07 |

Contents

Introduction

THE ART OF MULTIPLYING INFLUENCE

A CULTURE CRYING FOR LEADERSHIP

The local newspapers and national news media are continually address the need for leadership. It's the subject at the heart of every political candidacy and each congressional confirmation hearing. It's at stake in the evaluation of every sitting office-holder. People want to know: Does this person stand for worthy ideas? Does she have a character we can trust? Does he properly use resources to get the job done?

These questions aren't solely aimed at the government. Wherever we look today, our culture is crying for leadership.

Families need leaders. Our society is increasingly aware that we need parents who cultivate the character and gifts of their children, who establish healthy patterns of life, and who guide their families to make contributions beyond their own circle. Think how much of the oft-cited pain and fragmentation of family life could be repaired if parents were equipped for a deeper kind of leadership.

Businesses and civic organizations need leaders. Every headline trumpeting the latest corporate scandal or organizational failure reminds us that we need a new generation of leaders in the public square—people who discern worthy priorities, who use wise principles, and who have the internal life and skills to guide key organizations toward the fulfillment of their mission. Imagine the creative power that could be unleashed if these organizations were filled with the very best kind of leaders.

Churches and ministries need leaders. The church, parachurch ministries and Christian educational institutions have helped shape the kind of leaders needed in both the home and the public square. There is hardly a Christian ministry today, however, that does not desperately need quality people to provide the contexts where mature disciples and dynamic leaders get shaped. What might happen if the church and Christian ministries were able to contribute a new harvest of qualified leaders?

The need to fill the leadership deficit is the passion behind *Leadership Essentials*.

FIVE *PERSONAL* REASONS FOR THE LEADERSHIP DEFICIT

So why are we at a place of such deficit? Conversations with hundreds of people suggest the following factors in the reluctance to assume leadership:

- *Equipment shortage: "I haven't been equipped."* People feel ill-equipped to serve as leaders, and in some cases they are absolutely correct. The equipment manager didn't show up.

- *Description deficit: "I lack a clear job description."* People are unsure about what would actually be required if they got involved as leaders.

- *Image issue: "I'm not the leader type."* People have such an inflated sense of leadership or such a deflated sense of self that they don't perceive themselves as leaders or see what they have to offer.

- *Coaching crisis: "If only I had a mentor."* People have not been appropriately apprenticed to a leader who provides an up-close model of what leadership looks like and a step-by-step guide into the world of leading.

- *Passion problem: "I don't see the compelling need."* Some people would be willing to step forward to serve as leaders if they sensed an urgent need that could be addressed by their action.

FOUR *MINISTRY-BASED* REASONS FOR THE LEADERSHIP DEFICIT

Part of the reason we don't see more leaders rising up to meet the leadership needs of our time has to do with the way Christians "do" church or ministry.

- *Disciple-making gap: "Shouldn't I be a disciple first?"* The passion to be a leader flows out of the practice of being a disciple. Until our ministries become more intentional about forming the contexts and pathways by which lovers and learners of Jesus are made, it will be difficult to form leaders. Christian discipleship precedes Christian leadership.

  The curriculum *Leadership Essentials* is based on the assumption that both content and context are prerequisites for growing disciples. Leaders can only be made from disciples. A growing network of reproducing and multiplying discipleship groups serves as the "farm system" from which prospective leaders come.

- *Diversion dilemma: "No pastor has ever helped develop my leadership."* For years church staff members—particularly pastors—have been trained, have focused on and have been rewarded for "doing" ministry themselves. They have been diverted from the central biblical call of "developing" disciples and leaders, thinking, *If I pour myself into* developing *some people, where will I find the time to keep* doing *what all the other people expect?* Even where ministry staff recognizes the need for raising leaders, they often confess to feeling a lack of knowledge, tools or discipline to carry out that good intention.

- *Professionalism pitfall: "The ministry staff provides the leadership."* Many ministries find it difficult to raise leaders because of the professionalization of Christian ministry. Our culture's obsession with experts and credentials has seeped into the church and has created a perceived gulf of competence between professional staff and laypeople. This chasm is especially evident in larger ministries. Thus lay leaders often feel that they should leave leadership to the "pros."

- *Essence enigma: "I'm not entirely sure what being a leader means."* There is some significant confusion over what constitutes the essence of leadership. Is it, as some secular authorities suggest, the art of getting my way? Is leadership telling others what to do? Is it simply the discipline of holding meetings or drawing up strategic plans? Is leadership basically the business of increasing the ABCs—attendance, buildings and contributions—associated with an organization's life? Defining the essence of leadership remains something of an enigma.

ASSESS YOUR LEADERSHIP NEEDS

Take a few moments to assess the reasons for the leadership deficit in your context. The need provides the motivation to address the leadership concerns.

1. As you look back over the *personal* and *ministry-based* reasons for the leadership deficit, with which do you best identify?

2. Which of these deficits are evident in your ministry or organization?

WHAT DO WE MEAN BY CHRISTIAN LEADERSHIP?

At its most basic, leadership is influence; Christian leadership is Christlike influence.

In recent years the Christian community has wisely sought to correct some of the excesses of authoritarian and hierarchical leadership. It has become fashionable to speak of *servant leadership*.[1] This undoubtedly has been helpful, but it also has had some unintended side effects. Some people who have been placed in positions of significant responsibility are prepared for the servant part, but not the leader dimension. And because of the phrase "servant leadership," some genuinely gifted leaders are wary of being too assertive, lest they seem to be lacking in servant spirit.

The kind of leadership that *Leadership Essentials* will address tries to avoid the shoals of power play on the one hand and passivity on the other. It seeks to gather individuals and teams around a common mission or vision in order to combine their gifts to accomplish something bigger than they could do on their own.

The leadership we have in mind means Christian influence across the major institutions of our society. Therefore, it should not be restricted to what we think of as Christian ministry.

LEADERSHIP PROGRESSION

Though leadership at its most fundamental level is *influence* and therefore is not restricted to institutional roles, there is also a progressive way to think of leadership stages of development within Christian organizations or institutions.

1. *We start with making disciples.* This may seem like an obvious step, but making disciples—followers of Jesus—precedes and is foundational to Christlike leadership. This is the mission that Jesus assigned to the church when he told his disciples, "Go and make disciples [followers of me] of all nations" (Matthew 28:19). We get into trouble when we fail to move people toward Christlikeness and the disciplines of the faith as a prerequisite to leadership. When we skip this step, the distinctly Jesus-like quality of leadership is lost.

2. *Disciples become models for others to follow.* Jesus set the example by washing the disciples' feet. He put himself forth as an example and told his followers to do the same (John 13:1-17). The apostle Paul wrote, "Imitate me, just as I imitate Christ" (1 Corinthians 11:1 NLT). For many followers of Christ the sheer power of their life is influential, even if they don't have any clear strategy of reproduction or an overt destination they are trying to take people to.

3. *We make reproducing disciples.* Reproduction is built into the basic understanding of the identity of a disciple of Jesus. Disciples need to be taught how to reproduce or multiply their influence through others.[2]

4. *Gifted leaders build powerful teams.* Whether guiding a small discipleship group of three or four, leading a home Bible study of ten or being the point person for a strategic team that sets the pace for an organization that touches ten thousand, leadership is steering a group to use their spiritual gifts to accomplish an agreed-upon mission. There are many ways and styles to get to this point. Some team builders are administrators who help the team clarify their vision and marshal their resources to accomplish their mission. Others leaders are the heart of the mission, carrying the passion and keeping the vision alive by repeatedly bringing the group back to its primary reason for being.

5. *A few are anointed by God to make an extraordinary impact.* There are exceptionally powerful leaders that God raises up who have a five-star gift mix that sets them apart. Throughout Scripture God chose and used powerful leaders to send his people in new directions. Though this still happens, by definition these leaders are rare.

WHO IS THIS MATERIAL WRITTEN FOR?

Leadership Essentials is written for those who have been discouraged from entering into Christian leadership because of the personal and ministry-based reasons cited earlier and for existing leaders who hunger to lead more like Jesus. Specifically, it is intended to equip

- *Christian laypeople* desiring a basic understanding of the major principles and practices of Christian leadership, whether in the church, workplace, civic organization or family.

- *church or parachurch staff members* looking for a common, biblical framework for extending their influence.

IN WHAT CONTEXTS MIGHT THIS MATERIAL BE USED?

- *An existing leadership group.* To help a current group of ministry-team members (e.g., elders, church staff members, ministry or mission team) clarify their calling and move on to greater influence.

- *A leadership farm team.* To orient and stimulate a hand-picked group of potential leaders, preparing them for entry into formal leadership.

- *A mentoring relationship.* To spark learning and discussion between a mentor and an apprentice.

- *A small group or Bible class.* To catalyze the thinking and practice of a conventional group or class as they consider how their lives might have greater conformity to the example of Jesus and greater influence for the kingdom of God.

- *An aspiring individual.* To guide the growth of an individual seeking to develop his or her leadership influence.

HOW IS *LEADERSHIP ESSENTIALS* TO BE USED?

Each *Leadership Essentials* chapter has the following elements.

Core Truth. At the heart of each session is a carefully crafted nugget of truth that forms the central theme. Every element of the material that follows (memory verse, inductive Bible study, reading and leadership exercise) is simply an expansion on the core truth. Each session begins with participants discussing key words or phrases. This allows each person to enter the content on the same footing while also being able to discuss questions or issues that the core truth provokes.

Memory Verse. If you are familiar with *Discipleship Essentials,* you will note the same commitment to Scripture memory, but *Leadership Essentials* has lengthier segments. Scripture memorization is a worthy discipline. Because we have instant access to information through electronic media, we may not think we need to memorize anything. Yet our minds are our most powerful and present tool, and we must harness them as we develop our discipleship and leadership skills. Filling our minds with biblical wisdom and truth is the most important thing we can do. Memorizing Scripture is significant in shaping the way we perceive God's world.

Inductive Bible Study. Each session offers interaction with a key passage of Scripture. The passage centers the core truth within the context of God's Word. The inductive guides are intended to provoke deep thinking, not simply "filling in the blanks." In this section your opinions will be probed; then you will be encouraged to dig into the Word; and finally you will be directed to apply the truth to your life with rugged honesty.

Reading. The reading is designed to spell out in greater detail the core truth of the chapter. Each reading is rooted in the biblical vision, yet it is placed in our contemporary setting so that the real world informs our leadership development. Here the difference between Christian and secular leadership will be highlighted. The media consistently promotes material acquisition, fame, power and appearance as foundations to build our lives on. Christian leadership often contradicts the dominant culture's values. Therefore these readings challenge the contemporary milieu.

Leadership Exercise. Perhaps the most important element of each session is the leadership exercise. At the very least each session requires a personal application through guided reflection on the reading. Quite often, an actual task is crafted so that a leadership skill is put into practice and tested. It's not enough to simply think about leadership. We need to exercise our leadership "muscles" through practice.

HOW CAN I ADAPT *LEADERSHIP ESSENTIALS* FOR MY SETTING?

This material can be used in a variety of group settings to resource and develop leaders. The following are three suggested formats.

Preexisting leadership team. Leadership groups generally meet at regular intervals (such as monthly) with a ministry and business agenda to complete. You desire to balance the spiritual and growth dimensions of the personal and team life with the tasks to be accomplished. With a group of twelve or less, you can cover this material in forty-five-minute segments. Ask the leadership group to complete all the parts of the lessons, including the Scripture memory, prior to the meeting. Let them know that when you are together, you will pay special attention to the leadership exercise. The forty-five minutes could be divided this way:

Whole group discussion (10 minutes). (1) Taking the lesson as a whole, how would you summarize the totality of what this is all about? (2) Was there a particular truth or spiritual insight that spoke to you?

Break into triads or quads (groups of three or four, 30 minutes). (1) Recite the Scripture memory: what was the value for you of memorizing this particular Scripture? (2) Then turn to the Leadership Exercise and choose the questions or activities that would best speak to the development of your leaders and team.

Whole group closing (5 minutes). Solicit any insight or action steps from the triads/quads that could be beneficial for the whole leadership team to hear.

Special leadership group or small group format. Some of you will use this material to resource your leadership development track (leadership farm system) or an existing small group may choose to adopt this curriculum for a quarter. The assumption is that the group would be under twelve members. If you had 90-120 minutes of devoted time, the following is a suggested format:

Core truth (whole group discussion, 10 minutes). Ask the group to share the key words or phrases that spoke to them. What was the key truth or spiritual insight that spoke to them in the core truth?

Memory verses (pairs, 15 minutes). Recite the verses to each other and then interact over the inductive questions.

Bible study (whole group discussion, 25 minutes). Capture the highlights of the biblical passage by interacting over the inductive questions.

Leadership exercise (triads, 30 minutes). The group leader suggests which of the application questions and/or activities will do the most to expand the leadership character and capacity of the participants.

Closing (whole group, 10 minutes). Come back together for any closing remarks the leader desires to make and/or invite the participants to share where they were stretched or enhanced by the leadership exercise.

> "A CHRISTIAN LEADER IS A PERSON WITH A GOD-GIVEN CAPACITY AND THE GOD-GIVEN RESPONSIBILITY TO INFLUENCE A SPECIFIC GROUP OF GOD'S PEOPLE TOWARD GOD'S PURPOSE FOR THE GROUP."
>
> J. Robert Clinton, *The Making of a Leader*

Teaching or classroom setting. This curriculum could also be used in a more formal classroom setting where a teacher/trainer desires to intersperse their own biblical and leadership insights within the frame of the curriculum. If the leadership group is larger than twelve members, the following is the suggested format.

Introduction (pairs, 5 minutes). The group leader asks the participants to share in pairs their summary of what the lesson is all about. In addition, they are invited to share a key truth or spiritual insight that was particularly penetrating.

Core truth (5 minutes). The group leader highlights key words and phrases underscoring their importance to the central truth.

Memory verses (pairs, 15 minutes). Recite the verses to each other and then interact over the inductive questions.

Bible study (whole group, 25 minutes). The teacher/trainer uses the inductive guide for group interaction as well as adding their own research and insight to illumine the text.

Leadership exercise (triads or quads, 30 minutes). The teacher/trainer chooses from the menu of suggestions the application of the leadership content that is desired.

Closing (whole group, 10 minutes). The teacher/trainer asks the class members to share any growth steps that they experienced as a result of this lesson. Then a closing exhortation or reinforcement of a key truth can be offered. Finally, the teacher/trainer sets up the assignment for the next time the class will meet.

CONCLUSION

Leadership development is not simply a matter of completing some lessons and doing some exercises while engaging with others in honest interchange. This curriculum is a tool that provides the setting for potential transformation, but it's the Holy Spirit who grabs ahold of our hearts and changes our lives. So as we begin this journey may this be our prayer:

Dear Lord, as I begin this journey to grow into the leader you desire me to be, may you have your way with me. Give me the grace for honest self-examination and the energy to pursue the truth and implement the practices you would build into my life. Through Jesus Christ I pray, amen.

---

[1]Robert K. Greenleaf, *Servant Leadership,* 25th anniversary ed. (Mahwah, N.J.: Paulist Press, 2002). Since the late 1970s servant leadership has been a counter to the high-control, top-down management models of such theories as management by objectives.

[2]Greg's book *Transforming Discipleship* and its companion curriculum, *Discipleship Essentials,* describe the process of disciple-making reproduction and provide a curriculum to implement multiplying units.

Part One

THE CHARACTER OF A LEADER

We begin with the character of a leader for one simple reason: this is where the Scripture concentrates its focus. The New Testament, in particular, gives only minimal attention to what a leader does. Nowhere will you find any extensive job description for the role of pastor, elder or bishop. We come across only the thinnest references to teaching the truth (Acts 20:27-31; 1 Timothy 3:2; Titus 1:9) and equipping the saints for the work of ministry (Ephesians 4:11-12) as indicators of a leader's role. You won't discover a gifts checklist or a list of the top ten skills that a leader should have anywhere in the Bible.

The Bible is much more concerned about *who* a leader is than *what* a leader does. Why? New Testament leadership is about reflecting the character of *the* Leader and Shepherd of the flock, Jesus Christ. In the Pastoral Epistles (1-2 Timothy and Titus), Paul gives us lists of qualifications to be an elder in the church. With the exception of "apt to teach," all the qualifications are related to moral and spiritual character.

Therefore, in part one, we will study three characteristics of a leader.

Holy (chap. 1). Jesus Christ is the embodiment of the holy God and therefore our source and model for holy living. True leaders are reflectors. If Jesus is the sun, we are the moon, which can be seen only as it reflects a light that is not its own. Since we have no light of our own, we are reliant on making sure that we stay plugged into the One who is the source of light. Therefore, our first study looks at committing ourselves to cultivating the fruit of the Holy Spirit, the nine delicious character qualities that are simply a summary of the person of Jesus Christ.

Habitual (chap. 2). Christian leaders find true life and joy in the One they serve. They cultivate the rhythms and habits of a fruitful relationship with Christ that causes others to say, "The joy in that leader's life is something I want to have." This lesson examines how we can develop a training program that renews us so that "streams of living water will flow from within" us (John 7:38).

Humble (chap. 3). Good leaders exercise their power and influence properly. The worldly notion of power entails being dominant over others. Fear, intimidation and coercion are used to control. Jesus says, "Not so among us." Godly power does not exalt leaders but empowers those who are being served. In a word, the Christlike leader is *humble*.

1 / Holy

LOOKING AHEAD

Memory Verse: 1 Peter 1:14-19
Bible Study: Isaiah 6:1-8
Reading: Simply the Greatest
Leadership Exercise: Holiness Health Check

 Core Truth

What is the preeminent quality of Christ's character that informs the life of disciples who lead others?

Leading disciples* fix their gaze on the holiness of Christ and seek to reflect this holiness in the character and conduct of their own lives. This holiness is a blend of moral purity, spiritual produce, sacred purpose and transcendent power.

1. Identify key words or phrases in the question and answer above, and state their meaning in your own words.

2. Restate the core truth in your own words.

3. What questions or issues does the core truth raise for you?

---

*We use the phrase "leading disciples" throughout the book to describe the kind of leadership Christ calls us to. Leadership and discipleship are inexorably linked together. We must always see ourselves first as disciples of Christ and second as disciples who are called to lead.

Memory Verse Study Guide

Copy the entire text here:

Memory Verse: 1 Peter 1:14-19

Putting it in context: The apostle Peter was a man who had come face-to-face with his own sin. He had tried to talk Jesus out of going to the cross, bragged about how much more loyal he would be to Christ than the other disciples, and then bitterly denied Jesus when the pressure was on. Peter has also come face to face with God's amazing grace. This moves him to issue the very striking appeal in this text.

1. How could "ignorance" make a person "conform to . . . evil desires" (v. 14) or pursue an "empty way of life" (v. 18)? Give an example of this.

2. Based on your own experience or observations of others, what are some of the "evil desires" that might actually lurk behind the actions of someone in leadership?

3. What does the word *holy* (vv. 15-16) mean or suggest to you?

4. What does it mean to "live . . . as strangers here in reverent fear" (v. 17)?

5. List at least two arguments (more if you can) for being holy that Peter advances in this passage.

Inductive Bible Study Guide

Bible Study: Isaiah 6:1-8

Isaiah 6 recounts the calling of the prophet Isaiah into the service of God. The events we read about occur shortly after the death of Israel's beloved king, Uzziah. Up to that point Uzziah was the most formidable being that Isaiah had ever known. A brilliant statesman, uncommonly strong moral leader and winsome public figure, Uzziah had shepherded Israel for an unprecedented fifty years. When he died, all of Israel, including Isaiah, went into bitter mourning. Never again would they encounter such greatness. And then Isaiah was given this vision.

1. At Isaiah's time the great temple at Jerusalem would have been by far the largest, most glorious structure Isaiah had ever seen, especially since Uzziah had restored it. What does verse 1 suggest, however, about the magnitude and glory of God?

   What words are used to describe God's glory?

2. "Seraphs" were angelic warriors, beings of staggering strength and speed. In verse 4 we're told that the sound of their voices created a cataclysm of shock and awe in the temple. The reference to their "feet" is likely a euphemistic reference to "private parts." What do you think is the significance of these mighty beings covering up their eyes and "feet"?

3. What do the seraphs say about the character and influence of God in verse 3?

   What is the significance of their repeating "holy" three times?

4. What initial emotional and spiritual response did Isaiah have to this encounter (v. 5), and why?

Have you ever felt anything like this when contemplating God's nature? How do you relate to this experience of worship?

5. According to verses 6-7, how does the Lord alleviate Isaiah's sense of moral disintegration?

6. Why do you think Isaiah volunteered himself when God called (v. 8)?

7. What questions or issues does this passage raise for you?

👓 Reading: Simply the Greatest

The story is told of an older man who for many decades habitually returned every few years to the city of Athens. Upon each visit, he would climb to the top of the Acropolis, take a seat on one of its ancient stones and spend an hour or two letting his eyes wander over the massive pedestal, the soaring columns, and the perfect proportions of the Parthenon. When asked to explain the reason for this pattern, the elderly gentleman's eyes crinkled as he smiled: "I do this because it keeps my standards high."

For the same reason, many of us who hope to be used of God as leaders keep returning to gaze upon Jesus. He is the greatest possible standard for what it means to be a person and a leader. To be fair, claims like this have been made of others. When Vladimir Lenin was entombed in Moscow in 1924, the following inscription was placed next to his embalmed remains: "Here lies the greatest leader of all people of all time. He was the lord of the new humanity. He was the savior of the world."[1]

Those words, whether applied to Lenin or any other leader, ring hollow today, don't they? Those leaders lie dead and buried (or one day will). The clock is ticking, and their kingdoms are (or will be) history. Yet the person and influence of Jesus remains as alive today as the first day he stood on the temple mount of Jerusalem. As the twenty-first century was dawning, *Time* magazine made this observation:

> The memory of any stretch of years eventually resolves to a list of names, and one of the useful ways of recalling the past two millenniums is by listing the people who acquired great power. Muhammad, Catherine the Great, Marx, Gandhi, Hit-

ler, Roosevelt, Stalin and Mao come quickly to mind. There's no question that each of those figures changed the lives of millions and evoked responses from worship through hatred.

> It would require much exotic calculation, however, to deny that the single most powerful figure—not merely in these two millenniums but in all human history—has been Jesus of Nazareth. . . . [A] serious argument can be made that no one else's life has proved remotely as powerful and enduring as that of Jesus."[2]

Leadership is the art of multiplying influence, and by this standard Jesus must be considered the master artist. This is something of why so many of us agree with the writer to the Hebrews that Jesus is "worthy of greater honor" (Hebrews 3:3) than other leaders. Even those who cannot yet accept the core Christian claim that Jesus was the Creator of the universe, was made flesh (John 1:1-3, 14), cannot help but stand in awe or admiration before the brilliant ethical framework, the towering moral example, the enduring spiritual and social effects of the life and leadership of Jesus. The famed Briton H. G. Wells once wrote: "More than 1900 years later, a historian like myself, who doesn't even call himself a Christian, finds the picture centering irresistibly around the life and character of this most significant man. . . . The historian's test of greatness is 'What did he leave to grow?' Did he start men to thinking along fresh lines with a vigor that persisted after him? By this test, Jesus stands first."[3]

He is simply the greatest.

THE BEING OF THE BUILDER

But greatness can be a mysterious property. It is commonplace in our day to read books that reduce great leadership to a set of techniques or methodologies. Even Jesus has been commodified in this way, his leadership packaged into a neat set of practical utilities. We will certainly look closely at the practices of Jesus, but a careful study of the biblical materials that record Christ's life lead to an inescapable conclusion: Jesus was an exceptional *builder* because he was, first and foremost, an extraordinary *being. His influence was the effluence of his essence.* His impact was the overflow of his identity. His conduct was the outpouring of his character. And if we wish to follow him, we must begin with his *holiness.*

The word *holy* has fallen into disuse in our time. When used, it's often employed in a derogatory sense—as in "holy roller" or "holier than thou." For many people the word suggests a pinched, diminished or sanctimonious state of being. This is sad, because the biblical concept of holiness actually carries a vastly grander and more inspiring meaning. It is as different from the popular concept as the Parthenon is from an office cubicle. C. S. Lewis once commented to an American friend: "How little people know who think that holiness is dull. When one meets the real thing . . . it is irresistible. If even 10% of the world's population had it, would not the whole world be converted and happy before a year's end?"[4]

"PROFESSING CHRISTIANS MUST BE BROUGHT TO REALIZE THAT THE PREEMINENT DESIRE AND DEMAND OF GOD FOR US IS THAT OF THE CONTINUAL PURSUIT OF THE HOLINESS OF LIFE, AND THE REFLECTION OF HIS OWN HOLINESS."

Herbert S. Lockyer Sr., source unknown

When the Bible speaks of holiness it does so in a variety of colorful senses. All of these dimensions of holiness are vividly present in the character and conduct of Jesus. Together, they help to account for the fact that so many people found his leadership irresistibly influential.

THE PURITY OF JESUS (THE ABSENCE OF SIN)

In the most familiar sense, holiness is purity. It is a state of moral perfection. It is the utter absence of sin. It is living water running cold, clear and absolutely clean. This aspect of Jesus' character simply stupefied those who first spent time with him. Do you suppose individuals like Matthew (a tax collector) or Mary Magdalene (formerly demon-possessed) or the other disciples (working tradesmen) were naive about human nature? They certainly knew plenty about the superficiality, complexity and pretense of people. Some of them spent three years living in close quarters with Jesus. Yet the apostle Peter emerged saying of Jesus, "He committed no sin, and no deceit was found in his mouth" (1 Peter 2:22). The apostle John said, "In him is no sin" (1 John 3:5). The writer to the Hebrews summed up the consistent experience and teaching of Christ's first followers by saying that Jesus was "tempted in every way, just as we are—yet was without sin" (Hebrews 4:15).

How many of us could imagine saying something like this about one of our family members, college roommates or coworkers? How many of us could imagine a leader today saying to the press, "Go ahead, I dare you; see if you can find *any* dirt on me." Yet at one point Jesus faced off with some of the Pharisees who were bent on discrediting his leadership and said precisely this: "Can any of you prove me guilty of sin?" (John 8:46). Think how many leaders have had their influence diminished or cancelled out because, in spite of all they'd done or said, there was something hidden, something dark, some lack of integrity in their life. But no one could find any sin in Jesus. He was truly holy.

> "It is only when Christ is wholly Lord that we become whole ourselves."
>
> John Stott, from an address at Christ Church of Oak Brook

THE PRODUCE OF JESUS (THE PRESENCE OF FRUIT)

Holiness, however, is much more than the absence of sin. It is also the presence of glory. The space where the darkness and death of sin is not found is filled instead with the light and life of God. This is what the apostle John was getting at when he described breathlessly, on behalf of the other disciples, what they saw in Jesus: "The Word became flesh and made his dwelling among us. We have seen his glory, . . . full of grace and truth" (John 1:14).

The apostle Paul says that where the Holy Spirit of God resides, it drives out sin and replaces it with the resplendence of good fruit. "The fruit of the Spirit is love, joy, peace, patience, kindness, goodness, faithfulness, gentleness and self-control" (Galatians 5:22-23). These aspects of holiness are precisely the qualities we see abounding in Jesus. They help to explain why others were drawn to him like hungry people are drawn to a bowl of fruit.

Many people hunger for holiness without knowing it. For years I (Dan) asked people exploring church membership: "Do you want to be holy?" People shrugged their shoulders awkwardly. A few hands poked up shyly. Then I started asking, "Would you like a greater measure of love, joy, peace, patience, kindness, goodness and so on in your life?" Every hand in the room shoots up immediately. Every time.

It was this way with Jesus. His first followers saw in him a quality of character so attractive that they were willing to lay down their nets and follow him. They encountered a person so full of good fruit that they were pleased to go on a three-year-long road trip with him. They hoped, perhaps, to acquire more of such character through sheer contact with him. C. S. Lewis was right. Holiness, properly understood, is anything but dull. Holiness is the compelling beauty and fullness of God's own nature for which we were made.

THE PURPOSE OF JESUS (TOTAL DEDICATION)

The Bible also defines holiness in terms of being "set apart" or "dedicated to a sacred purpose." In the Old Testament certain *places,* like the tabernacle and temple, were regarded as "holy"; they were wholly dedicated to God's presence and service (Exodus 26:33). Likewise, the Israelites were commanded by God to set apart certain *possessions* to be solely used in the worship of God: "Anoint the altar of burnt offering and all its utensils; consecrate the altar, and it will be most holy" (Exodus 40:10). Setting apart certain environments and objects was a means of reflecting that God himself is distinct and separate from—transcendent—humanity. But it was also a means of recognizing that truly honoring God's glory and desires requires more than an occasional nod. It requires substantive dedication and commitment.

For these reasons the Jews also set apart or "made holy" *people* to God's purposes. Exodus 40 describes how the family of Aaron was consecrated to be God's priests. We read much later, in the Gospel of Luke, that "Joseph and Mary took [Jesus] to Jerusalem to present him to the Lord (as it is written in the Law of the Lord, 'Every firstborn male is to be consecrated to the Lord')" (Luke 2:22-23).

Jesus clearly lived with this sense of holiness too. Throughout his life, Jesus demonstrated a highly developed awareness of being set apart to fulfill God's will. In describing his purpose for being on earth, Jesus said, "I have come down from heaven not to do my will but to do the will of him who sent me" (John 6:38). When unpacking what really gave him a sense of fulfillment, Jesus said, "My food . . . is to do the will of him who sent me and to finish his work" (John 4:34). Summing up this unwavering sense of purpose, Jesus boldly declared, "I always do what pleases [my Father in heaven]" (John 8:29). And the writer of Hebrews affirmed, "[Jesus] was faithful to the one who appointed him" (Hebrews 3:2).

THE POWER OF JESUS (AWESOME POTENCY)

There is, however, a further dimension to holi-

> "CONSPICUOUS HOLINESS OUGHT TO BE THE MARK OF THE CHURCH OF GOD. A HOLY CHURCH HAS GOD IN THE MIDST OF HER."
>
> Charles Haddon Spurgeon, "Holiness, the Law of God's House"

ness that is very important. As we saw in our study of Isaiah 6, holiness is also often associated with God's awesome power. David Head, a Methodist churchman, points out that, regrettably, many miss this dimension as the following mock prayer reveals:

> Benevolent and easy-going [God], we have occasionally been guilty of errors of judgment. We have lived under the deprivations of heredity and the disadvantages of environment. We have sometimes failed to act in accordance with common sense. We have done the best we could in the circumstances, and have been careful not to ignore the common standards of decency. And we are glad to think that we are fairly normal. Do thou, O Lord, deal lightly with our infrequent lapses. Be thy own sweet Self with those who admit they are not perfect, according to the unlimited tolerance which we have a right to expect from thee. And grant as an indulgent parent that we may hereafter continue to live a harmless and happy life and keep our self-respect. Amen.[5]

It's difficult to read the Gospels and come away believing that the nature of Jesus is even remotely like this. Like the heavenly Father with whom the Spirit and Son are one, Jesus is no pale pushover. He will not be put in a convenient box for our purposes. He will not serve as anyone's on-tap resource or "Grace Bank" ATM. He cannot be conned, humored or manipulated. In no way does the presence of the fruit of the Spirit in Christ's life remove the reality that he is a being of awesome potency. Jesus is holy.

In the first chapter of Mark's Gospel we read just one of many encounters between Jesus and evil powers—powers so virulent that we would shudder to meet them in our nightmares. But notice how this dark force responds to Jesus: "What do you want with us, Jesus of Nazareth? Have you come to destroy us? I know who you are—the Holy One of God!" (Mark 1:24). The demons are afraid of Jesus. Others, even his own disciples, quaked as they saw Jesus' command over the very forces of nature: "They were terrified and asked each other, 'Who is this? Even the wind and the waves obey him!'" (Mark 4:41).

Jesus is not just auditioning for the job of "Lord"; he is the awesome, holy God who has come to meet us in the flesh and is still moving today through the power of his Holy Spirit. As theologian Karl Barth once observed: "One cannot speak of [Jesus], simply by speaking about man in a loud voice."[6] The God we meet in Christ weakens the knees of angels and demons alike, albeit for different reasons. Only by his amazing grace do we remain alive in his presence. Only by grace does he offer himself now to us as Savior before he returns one day as Judge. Only by his grace are we given an opportunity to play a part in the life of his kingdom.

THE PATH OF JESUS (STEPS TO HOLINESS)

Finally, in the kingdom of God, leadership is founded on *followership*. The apostle Peter ob-

> "JUST AS HE WHO CALLED YOU IS HOLY, SO BE HOLY IN ALL YOU DO; FOR IT IS WRITTEN: 'BE HOLY, BECAUSE I AM HOLY.'"
>
> 1 Peter 1:15-16

serves, Jesus "[left] you an example, that you should follow in his steps" (1 Peter 2:21). What does it look like for a Christian leader to follow in the holy path of Jesus? Four key imperatives come to mind.

Root out impurity. None of us will be perfectly holy in this life. Sin will continue to stain aspects of our character and conduct. As Christians we are grateful that God ultimately measures us not by the standard of our own righteousness but by Christ's. At the same time we remember that Jesus has "called us to a holy life" (2 Timothy 1:9). Our pursuit of purity is first and foremost a sign of our passion to be like the Master. It is also a major part of how we preserve our credibility as leaders. "We put no stumbling block in anyone's path, so that our ministry will not be discredited. Rather, as servants of God we commend ourselves in every way" (2 Corinthians 6:3-4). We can have tremendous natural gifts, all the right techniques and fine skills as a leader, but if we let pride, envy, gluttony, lust, anger, greed, sloth or some other sin to go unaddressed in us, our creative influence will be diminished or even cancelled. Leading disciples remember that purity is not the passion of prudes but the desire of those who want a life and legacy like Jesus'.

Cultivate the fruit of the Spirit. In chapter two we'll look at the habits by which the positive dimensions of a holy character get developed. Suffice it to say here that purposefully cultivating the fruit of the Spirit may be the most important thing leaders do. It is not just because people will bear with the imperfections and missteps of Christian leaders far more easily when those leaders exhibit the fruit, or because more people will want to come and stay at work alongside leaders who are holy in this sense, though both of these are true. Rather, this "produce" is far more influential than any program we turn out. When people meet true love, joy, peace and the like in the flesh, they are meeting the character and are drawing closer to the quality of Jesus himself. It is a leader's privilege to give people a taste of this communion.

Consecrate yourself daily. Jesus reveals that those who follow in his steps must be willing to be holy, that is, set apart and dedicated to God's purposes. To make the point forcefully, Jesus says: "If any want to become my followers, let them deny themselves and take up their cross daily and follow me" (Luke 9:23 NRSV). Christian leadership, then, is a daily and deliberate choice to pursue a path that will be very painful at times, but it also will have enor-

mous influence on others.

Remember before whom you stand and serve. Knowing a Lord of such awesome purity and potency keeps us properly accountable. We understand that "all authority in heaven and on earth" belongs to Jesus (Matthew 28:18) and whatever power or influence we are privileged to have in this life comes from him. One day he will fully review how we have handled the resources and relationships entrusted to us (Matthew 25:14-46). This same God expects to see his holy will done on earth as it is already is being done in heaven (Matthew 6:9-13). Thus, as his disciples who lead others, we handle our leadership with a blend of humble gratitude, trembling reverence and sacred purpose.

"Therefore, holy brothers, who share in the heavenly calling, fix your thoughts on Jesus" (Hebrews 3:1). Doing so, you'll find that it keeps your standards high.

[1]Raymond McHenry, *The Best of In Other Words* (Houston: Raymond McHenry, 1996), p. 221.
[2]Reynolds Price, "Jesus of Nazareth," *Time,* December 6, 1999 <www.time.com/time/magazine/article/0,9171,992745-1, 00.html>.
[3]Mark Link, S.J., *He Is the Still Point of the Turning World* (Chicago: Argus Communications, 1971), p. 111.
[4]C. S. Lewis, *Letters to an American Lady* (Grand Rapids: Eerdmans, 1967), p. 19.
[5]David Head, *He Sent Leanness: A Book of Prayers for the Natural Man* (New York: Macmillan, 1962).
[6]Karl Barth, *The Word of God and the Word of Man* (Boston: Pilgrim Press, 1928), pp. 195-96.

Leadership Exercise: Holiness Health Check

1. What aspect of Jesus' character do you find particularly compelling?

2. Take a moment to do a fearless moral inventory of the purity of your character. List at least two things in you which, if left unaddressed, might be a stumbling block to those who follow your lead.

3. Evaluate the presence of the fruit of the Spirit in your life. Check the box next to the fruits you feel are most abundant in your life right now.

   ____ *Love.* I desire the good of others and express this in my actions, seeking to love others as Christ loves me.

   ____ *Joy.* I remain content, hopeful and thankful, even in the midst of difficult circumstances.

   ____ *Peace.* I release anxiety about the past, present and future by putting my faith in God's presence, promises and providence.

   ____ *Patience.* I demonstrate forbearance in the face of others' sins, fears and limitations, knowing that God does this with me.

   ____ *Kindness.* I show practical consideration and compassion toward others, meeting needs in ways felt by them.

   ____ *Generosity.* I use my resources as I believe Jesus would, expressing to God and extending to others my sense of the grace I've been given.

   ____ *Faithfulness.* I remain true to God's Word and calling, keeping my promises and persevering in the face of trials.

   ____ *Gentleness.* I exhibit sensitivity and tenderness in my treatment of others, restraining the force I could exercise.

   ____ *Self-control.* I demonstrate power, through the Spirit, to direct my passions and appetites rather than having them direct me.

4. Circle any of the fruit listed (in number 3) that you particularly sense needs to be growing in you. Offer a prayer to God right now, that he would help you cultivate greater abundance of fruit in these areas.

5. What aspects of your life do you regard as *holy*—set apart or consecrated—to God?

How does this show?

6. What are you still holding back—unwilling or not yet able to dedicate to God?

Going Deeper
Jerry Bridges, *The Pursuit of Holiness,* Colorado Springs: NavPress, 1988.
Memorize Colossians 3:1-17.

2 / Habitual

LOOKING AHEAD

Memory Verse: 1 Corinthians 9:24-27
Bible Study: Mark 4:1-20
Reading: Training Versus Trying to Live the Christian Life
Leadership Exercise: Developing a Rhythm for Life

 Core Truth

How do Christian leaders cultivate holiness?

Leading disciples plow furrows in the soil of their hearts in order that the implanted seed of God's Word can take root and bear much fruit. These furrows are created through the classic spiritual disciplines (habits) that prepare and open the inner life so that the Holy Spirit can do his transformative work.

1. Identify key words or phrases in the question and answer above, and state their meaning in your own words.

2. Restate the core truth in your own words.

3. What questions or issues does the core truth raise for you?

> "SPIRITUAL FORMATION IN CHRIST IS THE PROCESS BY WHICH ONE MOVES AND IS MOVED FROM SELF-WORSHIP TO CHRIST-CENTERED SELF-DENIAL AS A GENERAL CONDITION OF LIFE IN GOD'S PRESENT AND ETERNAL KINGDOM."
>
> Dallas Willard, *Renovation of the Heart*

Memory Verse Study Guide

Copy the entire text here:

Memory Verse: 1 Corinthians 9:24-27

Living as a Christian and preparing for leadership is dependent on adopting a disciplined lifestyle. In our memory verses Paul compares the discipline of growing in Christ to an athlete in training for competition.

1. *Putting it in context:* Look at 1 Corinthians 9:1-23. How is Paul's commitment to the gospel an extended illustration of a leader who is in "strict training" (v. 25)?

2. What is the main point Paul wants us to grasp in comparing the Christian life to that of an athlete?

3. In verse 25 Paul contrasts the goal of an athletic competition with the goal of the Christian life. How should this affect our motivation?

4. At present, how would you characterize your attitude or approach to living the Christian life?

5. What change in attitude are you being asked to adopt by this Scripture?

Inductive Bible Study Guide

Bible Study: Mark 4:1-20

Jesus' clear intention for our lives is that we bear much fruit (John 15:8). The fruit he has in mind is both quantitative (more disciples) and qualitative (better disciples). Since fruit is organic, farming is often the best image to help us understand how this occurs. In this parable Jesus teaches us that soil readiness is the all-important variable in fruit bearing. He seems to indicate that we have something to do with preparing the soil of our lives—so the seed of God's Word can have its natural effect.

1. Jesus describes four kinds of soil, which appear to be varied conditions of the heart. Three of these soils are resistant in different ways to the seed of God's Word. The first of these is *hard soil* (vv. 4, 15). What is the condition of this heart?

   What does this look like in contemporary life?

2. The second soil is *shallow soil* (vv. 5-6, 16-17). What does it mean for a life not to have deep roots?

   What exposes the shallow nature of the roots?

   Can you illustrate from personal observation?

3. The third soil is *thorny soil* (vv. 7, 18-19). Discuss the causes Jesus mentions for choking out the new growth.

   A. "worries of this life"

   B. "deceitfulness of wealth"

   C. "desires for other things"

4. The fourth soil is *good soil* (vv. 8, 20). What can we do to prepare the soil of our lives so the seed of God's Word can have its full, reproductive effect?

If preparing the good soil addresses the qualities of the bad soils, how would you go about addressing the hard, shallow and thorny parts of your life?

Which needs greatest attention?

5. What questions or issues does this passage raise for you?

"SPIRITUAL DISCIPLINES ARE THE MAIN WAY WE OFFER OURSELVES TO GOD AS A LIVING SACRIFICE. . . . GOD THEN TAKES THIS SIMPLE OFFERING OF OURSELVES AND DOES WITH IT WHAT WE CANNOT DO, PRODUCING WITHIN US DEEPLY INGRAINED HABITS OF PEACE, LOVE AND JOY IN THE HOLY SPIRIT."

Richard Foster, *Celebration of Discipline*

Reading: Training Versus Trying to Live the Christian Life

Most Christians are *trying* rather than *training* to live the Christian life, writes John Ortberg. What is the difference? A "trying" mentality is what you do when you dabble, when you take "a shot" at something new. When presented with a fresh challenge, we might say, "I am going to give it a try." A trying mentality is often evidenced by our response to a sermon. The preacher exhorts us to be more patient, so we resolve to control our temper around an irritating three year old, or to be more tolerant of a work associate whose personality sends up a wall. Trying only gets us to Tuesday.

There are many areas of life where a trying mentality will just not cut it. No one wakes up on a Saturday morning, opens the newspaper, notices that there is a marathon being run that day and then says, "Hey, I'm not doing anything today, I think I will give it a try." Months of careful preparation are needed to propel oneself over a twenty-six-mile course, no matter what the pace may be. Ortberg concludes, "Learning to think, feel, and act like Jesus is at least as demanding as learning to run a marathon or play the piano."[1]

For some reason we have come to expect that following Jesus should be relatively easy. We know that in other realms of life disciplined effort is necessary to achieve anything worthwhile, but we have not applied the same, let alone higher, standards to our becoming Christlike followers, much less leaders.

The Christian life needs to be approached in the same way that an athlete trains to compete. Practice, discipline, repetition, routine. In his prime, Michael Jordan routinely pulled off victories at the end of games. Why? Because he simply tried harder at the end of a game?

No. He was able to do in the game what he had practiced ad nauseum in the gym. He spent countless hours out of the public eye grooming his jump shot and free throws until they became automatic.

IMAGES OF THE DISCIPLINED LIFE

The apostle Paul often turns to the image of an athlete when describing the training of a disciple: "Do you not know that in a race all the runners run, but only one gets the prize? Run in such a way as to get the prize. Everyone who competes in the games goes into strict training. They do it to get a crown that will not last; but we do it to get a crown that will last forever" (1 Corinthians 9:24-25).

Note the *how much more* line of argument Paul uses here. In human athletic competition a person receives accolades in the moment, but these are fleeting and fading. Who remembers who won last year, let alone years ago? But we are after a crown that will last forever, therefore *how much more* we should train to reflect the One we follow.

Images of a disciplined life dominate the New Testament. Paul compares our life to a *builder* who must choose quality materials to build on the foundation of Jesus Christ. Will we choose wood, hay or straw that will not make it through the fire of judgment, or will we build with precious metals (1 Corinthians 3:10-15)? Just prior to Paul's death, he exhorts Timothy, his son in the faith, to accept the baton of the gospel that he is passing on to him. He urges Timothy, in the face of opposition, to be strong in the grace of our Lord. Then Paul piles up accessible images of strength that should shape Timothy's attitude toward the faith. (1) Obey the Lord like a *soldier* under the authority of commanding officer. (2) Be disciplined like a victorious *athlete* who competes according to the rules. (3) Follow the example of *hardworking farmers* who receive the fruit of their labors (2 Timothy 2:3-6).

In other words, to be a winsome follower of Jesus Christ we must adopt a rigorous training program. It takes even more effort and discipline to be conformed to the likeness of Jesus Christ than it does to complete a graduate degree, become a brain surgeon or be an accomplished musician. To be good at anything requires a "long obedience in the same direction."[2] Now transfer this to the way you approach being a follower of Christ.

A *training* mentality develops and practices godly *habits*. In writing to the Ephesians Paul says: "You were taught, with regard to your former way [habits] of life, to put off [continuously, daily] your old self, which is being corrupted by its deceitful desires; . . . and to put on [continuously, daily] the new self, created to be like God in true righteousness and holiness" (Ephesians 4:22, 24). The image is that of taking off an old set of soiled garments (those old habits) and putting on fresh attire that reflect the glistening life of God.

Paul repeatedly uses the *principle of replacement* as the way to acquire godly habits. Lest we miss the initial point, he gives us five more illustrations: (1) put off falsehood and put on truthfulness (v. 25); (2) put off lingering anger and put on quick resolve (vv. 26-27); (3) put off stealing and put on hard work (v. 28); (4) put off unwholesome talk and put on that which

builds up (v. 29); (5) put off bitterness, rage and anger, and put on gracious speech (vv. 31-32). Every day the battle within is the same: What do I need to continuously put off so that I can replace it with God-pleasing habits?

We call this practicing the *spiritual disciplines*. Spiritual disciplines are the habits or practices that prepare us for the transformative work of the Holy Spirit. Now, it might appear that we can produce our own spiritual change by simply incorporating the right habits or spiritual disciplines in our life. John Ortberg again helps us understand the role of spiritual disciplines through contrasting metaphors. Consider the difference, he says, between piloting a motor boat and a sailboat. A motorboat is propelled by its own power, and similarly we can attempt to operate our lives by ourselves. But the Christian life is has much more in common with a sailboat. The sailboat relies on the wind, which blows where it wills. As operator of the sailboat, we can steer the rudder and erect the sails, but we can't cause the wind to blow. Spiritual disciplines are like the sails hoisted to catch the wind of the Spirit. In other words, by themselves the spiritual disciplines don't yield transformation into Christlikeness, but they put us in the position to be encountered by God, who is the life-changer.

> "SPIRITUAL TRANSFORMATION IS NOT A MATTER OF TRYING HARDER, BUT TRAINING WISELY."
>
> John Ortberg, *The Life You've Always Wanted*

APPLYING VIM WITH VIGOR

Dallas Willard uses the acronym VIM to describe a reliable pattern of transformation for the follower of Christ.[3]

Catch the Vision. First, a disciple must have

vision. The Christian leader's vision is centered on the picture of a holy, Christlike life, a life in the kingdom of God (see chap. 1). Willard suggests that there are two major objectives in growth toward Christlikeness. The first objective brings us to the place where we "dearly love and constantly delight in that 'heavenly Father' made real in Jesus and are quite certain that there is no limit to the goodness of his intentions or his power to carry them out. . . . When the mind is filled with this great and beautiful God, the natural response, once all inward hindrances are removed, will be to do 'everything I have told you to do.' "[4]

Develop the Intention. This vision of holiness naturally leads to developing the *intention* or the will to live in this kingdom reality. Intention is the decision to obey or to live consistently with the reality of the kingdom life, to intentionally adopt this vision as our reality. But how do we do this? It must be accompanied by the means or disciplines that structure our spirit life.

The second objective, therefore, of "a curriculum for Christlikeness" is to align our bodies with the work of the Holy Spirit. Paul tells us to present our bodies as a "living sacrifice," which is our "spiritual act of worship" (Romans 12:1). Athletes perform the same drills over and over until their bodies have learned to respond automatically. In athletic circles this is known as "muscle memory." Spiritual disciplines form *spiritual* muscle memory. The goal of the automatic response built into our bodies over time is to feel, think and act like Jesus. Ortberg writes, "Following Jesus simply means learning from him to arrange my life around activities that enable me to live in the fruit of the spirit. Spiritual disciples are to life what practice is to the game."[5]

Take hold of the Means. To accomplish the objective of making our bodies extensions of the Holy Spirit's impulses, Willard says that we must break "the power of patterns of wrongdoing and evil that govern our lives because of our long habituation to a world alienated from God."[6] How do we do this? We must unlearn the bad habits of spiritual muscle memory and teach ourselves God-pleasing habits of spiritual muscle memory through the disciplines of abstinence and engagement.

We become sensitive to the "patterns of wrongdoing and evil" within us through the primary *disciplines of abstinence:* solitude and silence. Solitude involves extended periods apart from human contact, which is enhanced by silence, the removal of distracting noises and sounds that fill our lives. Why are these two so primary? As we settle into quiet, the automatic responses of our heart surface and we get in touch with what is generally hidden from us. "The grip of the usual must be broken," says Willard. Ruth Haley Barton, author of *Invitation to Solitude and Silence,* uses an image that was given to her by her spiritual director at a silent retreat. She arrived harried to the retreat center and was having considerable difficulty settling into the quiet. Her spiritual director there told her that her life was like "a jar of rushing river water." She was living her life at such a pace that she had become a murky mixture. Only as she settled into the silence would the silt settle to the bottom of the jar and would the water of her life become clear.[7] Only as a person settles into the quiet can the dirt begin to drift to the bottom of the jar so that the water becomes clear.

The disciplines of abstinence then prepare us for the *disciplines of engagement.* Solitude and silence open us to the penetration of the Word of God through study. These disciplines are like the plow that cuts furrows in the hard soil of our hearts. We can then allow the seed of the Word to fill our mind and spirit, which then begins to shape our automatic responses. "Once solitude has done its work, the key to this progression is study. Place our minds fully upon God and his kingdom (Vision). Study brought to natural completion is worship."[8] Willard notes that study is not the same as gathering information. Instead, it's the internalization of the character of God so that it influences our bodily responses of thought, feeling and action. Studying the goodness of God, for example, will naturally lead to *worship*. Worship is the completion of study. The apostle Paul spontaneously breaks out in a benediction at the end of Romans 11 after he has contemplated the grand of scheme of God's redemption. He can't contain his worship: "Oh, the depth of the riches of the wisdom and knowledge of God!" (Romans 11:33).

Adopting a training paradigm requires structuring our lives around the *means* that will keep the *vision* of the good and sovereign God before us and the *intention* to conform our lives to this reality.

STRENGTHENING A LEADER'S SOUL

I (Greg) had an experience that led to reordering and reprioritizing my leadership. It was the summer of 1993 and I was given the gift of a sabbatical after five years as senior pastor. Since this was my first sabbatical, I did not know exactly how best to use the time. A member of the church I served challenged me to go away on a three-day silent retreat. This sounded like something I should do on a sabbatical, but, frankly, I approached this time more with fear than fascination. I thought, *What would I do for long unstructured periods of quiet? Would I be bored silly after an hour with another seventy-one hours before me? Meals, the ultimate social context, in silence?*

The habit of reflection. Yet I took up the challenge and checked myself into a nearby retreat center. Being an agenda-driven person I went away with a question, "Lord, what is your vision for the church for the next five years?" It seemed like an appropriate question. After all, I was charged with leadership as senior pastor. Leaders need vision. Leadership certainly is in large measure leading people somewhere. It might be a good idea to lead people where the Lord wanted them to go. Yet in the extended quiet under shade trees and leisurely strolls, the Lord serendipitously interrupted me. Gently, I heard the Lord say to me, "Greg, you have the wrong question. The question is not, What is my vision for you? but, What is your vision of me?" Now that is a very different question!

This question has fascinated me ever since. For it caused me to look at my life in a way that I had not dared to entertain. I had to ask myself, *What does my life communicate to others about the God that I claim to serve and repre-*

> "IN SILENCE WE NOT ONLY WITHDRAW FROM THE DEMANDS OF LIFE IN THE COMPANY OF OTHERS BUT ALSO ALLOW THE NOISE OF OUR THOUGHTS, STRIVINGS AND COMPULSIONS TO SETTLE DOWN SO WE CAN HEAR A TRUER AND MORE RELIABLE VOICE."
>
> Ruth Haley Barton, *Invitation to Solitude and Silence*

sent? I frankly did not like what I saw. The message I was receiving back from others was, You are intense and unapproachable. I was a driven person, and in the process I was driving others to fulfill the vision I had for the church. Outside my conscious awareness, people had too readily become mere tools to fulfill my aspirations.

Once I opened myself to self-examination, a whole set of questions started to cascade upon me: *What was my life speaking* (to paraphrase Parker Palmer)? *Was I experiencing and conveying joy in my relationship with Christ?* I had to conclude that if others were asked to describe me, very few people would have listed the quality of joy. Then it hit me. *What was the point if my life did not convey that I was finding pleasure in my relationship with Christ? Programs, plans, goals, dreams, budgets, buildings—for what purpose?*

The habit of sabbath. I came back from my sabbatical with the intent to live at a different pace and structure my life in a way that lived out of the fullness of Jesus Christ. This meant two spiritual disciplines had to be implemented immediately, and as far as humanly possible become part of my rhythm. The first was to establish a weekly sabbath. I had violated that practice to my peril, as I observe most Christian leaders do today. Work readily intruded into my designated day off. It was hard for me to disconnect. A true sabbath means ceasing from labor and resting. I made the commitment to make one day a week a work-free space.

I was determined to not have my identity become coequal with my role as a leader. I am not my work, even if it *is* a calling. I am first and foremost a beloved child of the Father, and I want to live under the pleasure of the Father as well as give him pleasure with my life. This

meant that I would do those things on my sabbath that were life-giving to me. This usually meant starting the day in some reflective study unrelated to sermon preparation. It might even mean a little writing, since that generally added value to the experience. I also took up biking. I found that putting on my helmet, hopping on my mountain bike and churning up dust along the railroad tracks was about as exhilarating as could be.

To implement the sabbath routine, though, meant taking a major step of faith. For me to truly get an uninterrupted sabbath, I needed to shift my day off from Friday to Thursday. The major obstacle to this shift was the completion of my sermon. I will confess that I am obsessive when it comes to this task. I cannot rest until it is done. I am like a bulldog when it comes to wrestling a sermon to the ground. But because of the flow of the week, if I were to shift my day off to Thursday, this would mean I would have to set aside the message preparation on Thursday and return to complete it on Friday. Given my structured personality, would I be able to be free from its nagging attention to truly be renewed? Therefore, to embrace a sabbath was both a major act of trust and obedience if I was to going to live a sane and renewable life consistent with God's intended pattern.

I found God to be faithful. I was given the grace to set aside what would normally be nagging at my mind all week long. The Lord presented the question of trust and obedience to me as a personal challenge: Greg, can you trust me to be faithful to the teaching of my Word if you are living in a way that is consistent with the instructions in my Word?

The habits of silence and solitude. I also came back from my summer sabbatical committed to practicing a thirty-six to forty-eight hour quarterly silent retreat. My first experience had been so revolutionary that I knew this needed to be part my long-term rhythm. So into the calendar it went, planned on those weeks when I was not preaching on the following Sunday. This again was no easy task. It seemed that Mondays and Tuesdays were the best time for this, yet it was the time of the regular weekly staff meeting and worship-team preparation for the following Sunday. There was always something that could intrude on this sacred space. Yet it was because of the anticipated island of respite in my calendar that I carefully guarded the time. I came to regard this as a time of "unhurried solitude." *Unhurried,* what a counterculture quality! Once the practice became routine, I learned how to settle in more quickly and embrace the quiet.

The habits of meditation and journaling. I regularly stored up matters of complexity that I needed to bring to the Lord to ponder in prayer and reflect on in my journal. The things that seemed so complex became much simpler in solitude. I would be prompted in quiet to pay attention to people I had passed by too quickly in the normal course of life. I enjoyed a leisurely walk with a hymnbook in hand, singing to my Lord. Extended portions of Scripture could be consumed in one sitting

rather than just a paragraph or two in the daily battle for a few moments of silence. Invariably, upon my return I would feel refreshed with a much clearer perspective of what I should be about. Then in the days that followed I could sense a warmth and life being emitted from my being. It was as if I was a rock that had absorbed the sun, and when night came I simply radiated back what had been stored up.

BRINGING IT HOME

The question that continues to address any Christian leader is, What does your life convey about your joy in Jesus Christ? Are you finding joy in your relationship with him? Are you living in such a way that you have structured time that allows you to remain in love with him? In the book of Revelation, Jesus' message to the church at Ephesus was, "I hold this against you: You have forsaken your first love" (Revelation 2:4). Can that be said of you? You may have caught a *vision* of the character of Christ. You may have an *intention* to become a leader like him. But what *means* do you use to guard and cultivate this primary relationship out of which Christian leadership flows? What is the point if people don't see us enjoying our relationship with Christ? And what is the point if we are not enjoying it?

---

[1]John Ortberg, *The Life You've Always Wanted* (Grand Rapids: Zondervan, 1997) pp. 47-48.
[2]Thanks to Eugene Peterson for popularizing this observation by Friedrich Nietzsche. See Peterson's *A Long Obedience in the Same Direction* (Downers Grove, Ill.: InterVarsity Press, 2000).
[3]Dallas Willard, *Renovation of the Heart* (Colorado Springs: NavPress, 2002), p. 85.
[4]Dallas Willard, *The Divine Conspiracy* (San Francisco: HarperSanFrancisco, 1998), p. 321.
[5]Ortberg, *Life You've Always Wanted,* pp. 48-49.
[6]Willard, *Divine Conspiracy,* p. 341.
[7]Ruth Haley Barton, *Invitation to Solitude and Silence* (Downers Grove, Ill.: InterVarsity Press, 2004), p. 29.
[8]Willard, *Divine Conspiracy,* p. 361.

Leadership Exercise: Developing a Rhythm for Life

A life of spiritual disciplines and practices can help us make ourselves available to God for the work that only the Holy Spirit can do. But spiritual disciplines in themselves do not ensure a God encounter. They simply put us into a position where we are open to whatever the Lord would say to us.

The following exercise will help you develop a plan that will prepare you for a life of discipleship.* This plan must be *personal.* It must work for you and should not simply copy someone else's practice. It also should be *balanced.* This means establishing daily, weekly, monthly, quarterly and annual rhythms. It also must be *realistic.* What works for a single adult will be very different from that of a parent with young children. Finally, your plan should be *flexible.* Life happens. Keep experimenting to see what works for you.

In order to craft a plan, contemplate your answers to following questions.

1. *Desire.* To the invalid by the pool of Bethesda, Jesus asked, "Do you want to get well?" (John 5:6). To the blind beggar Bartimaeus, Jesus asked, "What do you want me to do for you?" (Mark 10:51).

   • Translate your current longings for God into a word, phrases, sentences, images or metaphors that capture your desire for spiritual transformation.

   • Pay attention to your experiences and practices that lead you to feel close to God. Are there particular practices that seem to open you to God? What are these?

2. *Powerlessness.* "My dear children, for whom I am again in the pains of childbirth until Christ is formed in you" (Galatians 4:19).

   • In what areas are you most aware of your need for transformation and your powerlessness to bring it about?

3. *Plan.* "Continue to work out your salvation with fear and trembling, for it is God who works in you to will and to do according to his good purpose" (Philippians 2:12-13).

   • What practices or disciplines would you like to incorporate into your life?

   Daily. How much time is available? When? Where will you meet God?

---

*I (Greg) am indebted to Ruth Haley Barton and Adele Ahlberg Calhoun for their input in shaping this exercise.

Weekly sabbaths. Can you see yourself declaring a work-free space and doing only those things that restore life to you? Why or why not? What would it take for you to get to this place? Dream about how you would fill this day to "restore your soul."

Monthly or quarterly. What practices would allow you to live as an attentive disciple of Christ? These practices usually consist of lengthier periods of solitude and silence or the disciplines of engagement and service.

Annually. What practices would open your heart to God that might only fit into an annual rhythm?

_____ conference

_____ short-term mission trip

_____ silence and solitude retreat

_____ local service project

_____ covenant group

_____ other _____

- What further action steps will be necessary to implement these rhythms?
  Daily

  Weekly

  Monthly/quarterly

  Annually

- Who do you need to help you craft your "rhythm of life," and with whom will you share your plan?

    _____ *Spiritual friend:* a mutual partner of the heart

    _____ *Spiritual director:* a trained guide who can hear and reflect back what he or she sees God doing in your life

    _____ *Mentor:* someone you hold in high regard and after whom you desire to learn and pattern your life

3 / Humble

LOOKING AHEAD

Memory Verse: Matthew 7:1-5
Bible Study: Philippians 2:1-11
Reading: He Must Increase, I Must Decrease
Leadership Exercise: Keep Watch Over Your Heart

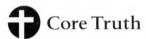 Core Truth

What is the primary ambition of Christian leaders?

Leading disciples are ambitious to advance the fame and reputation of Christ and his kingdom. Knowing that ambition can be diverted to self-exaltation and pride of accomplishment, a circumspect attitude must be adopted. Proper motivation is so important that Christian leaders place themselves in a relational setting where they are regularly asked about the condition of their soul.

1. Identify key words or phrases in the question and answer above, and state their meaning in your own words.

2. Restate the core truth in your own words.

3. What questions or issues does the core truth raise for you?

Memory Verse Study Guide

Copy the entire text here:

Memory Verse: Matthew 7:1-5

The flipside of humility is pride. One of the evidences of pride is our tendency to judge others with a harsher standard than we judge ourself. To justify ourself we find fault with others. In our memory verse Jesus calls us to shift the emphasis to self-examination before we correct others.

1. In verses 1-2 Jesus commands, "Do not judge." How do you think Jesus is using the term *judge?*

2. Is there a place for evaluating and correcting someone else's behavior? If so, how might this differ from judging?

3. What is the reason that Jesus gives for not judging?

4. How do verses 3-5 support the reasons for not judging stated in verses 1-2?

5. Jesus seems to be saying, "It is a law of life that we consistently underestimate the size of our own faults and overestimate the size of others'. We all tend to judge in our own favor." Do you think this is true? Why or why not?

6. Where do you see this tendency in yourself?

7. Are there particular areas where you find yourself hard on others? Why do you think this is?

8. On what basis can we point out an area of correction in another person's life?

Inductive Bible Study Guide

Bible Study: Philippians 2:1-11

This is a classic New Testament text on the practice and model of humility. We could title this passage "The Descent of a Leader." Paul calls the Philippian community to a unity that is grounded in an attitude of humility. He then plays the ultimate motivational trump card by turning to the model of Jesus Christ, who gave up his glory to become one with us. Is there any greater motivator than the model of Jesus himself?

1. In verses 1-2 Paul appeals for unity. On what does he base his appeal?

2. In verse 3 Paul first defines humility by what we are to avoid. Put each of these phrases in your own words and give an example:

   "selfish ambition":

   "vain conceit":

3. In verses 3-4 Paul gives us the definition of humility in two parts. What would this look like in your life?

   "Consider others better than yourselves." In what sense do you think Paul is using the word *better?*

   "Look not only to your own interests, but also the interests of others." How do we best become aware of the interests of others?

4. According to verses 6-7, what did Jesus Christ give up and what did he take on?

5. What do you suppose it required of Jesus to humble himself—even to the point of death on the cross (v. 8)? Ponder this reality.

6. Summarize what you think Paul wants us to grasp about the nature of the humble life.

7. What was the reward of humility for Jesus?

    Is there a parallel with us?

8. What questions or issues does this passage raise for you?

"WHEN HUMILITY DELIVERS A MAN FROM ATTACHMENT TO HIS OWN WORDS AND HIS OWN REPUTATION, HE DISCOVERS THAT TRUE JOY IS ONLY POSSIBLE WHEN WE HAVE COMPLETELY FORGOTTEN OURSELVES. AND IT IS ONLY WHEN WE PAY NO MORE ATTENTION TO OUR LIFE AND OUR OWN REPUTATION AND OUR OWN EXCELLENCE THAT WE ARE AT LAST COMPLETELY FREE TO SERVE GOD FOR HIS SAKE ALONE."

Thomas Merton, quoted in Tim Hansel, *Through the Wilderness of Loneliness*

Reading: He Must Increase, I Must Decrease

"He must become greater; I must become less" (John 3:30). John the Baptist's words encapsulate the attitude of leading disciples.

John's relationship to Jesus and his role in the kingdom as a herald and a forerunner of Jesus serve as an excellent model for us. John shows us what true humility looks like and how to avoid the pitfalls of pride.

John's humility is quite remarkable when you consider the human dynamics. Does anyone ever willingly give up the crowds' adulation? Yet this is exactly what John did. Mark tells us that "the whole Judean countryside and all the people of Jerusalem went out to him" (Mark 1:5). God's silence in Israel was broken through John's voice. It had been four hundred years since God had spoken through the prophet Malachi. Now God was speaking again through this rather strange figure. The famine of God's word was over. The people flocked in mass to hear John's message of repentance and preparation. The rule of thumb is that once the chorus of exaltation begins, it inevitably goes to our head. Popularity leads to power. We begin to think we are bigger than we really are. If there is one aphorism that has proven to be inviolable, it is Lord Acton's dictum, "Power tends to corrupt, and absolute power corrupts absolutely."

Yet John the Baptist exits stage right when Jesus, the leading man, takes his place on center stage. How was this possible, and what are the lessons for us?

First Lesson

John's clear sense of his call defined his identity (John 1:19-28; 3:27-29). He was inwardly rooted by the truth. John's powerful message authoritatively delivered raised the question about who he was. The religious leaders asked him, "Are you Elijah? . . . Are you the Prophet [meaning Messiah]? . . . Who are you? Give us an answer to take back to those who sent us. What do you say about yourself?" (John 1: 21-23). John had said from the beginning, "I am not the Christ. . . . But among you stands one you do not know. He is the one who comes after me, the thongs of whose sandals I am not worthy to untie" (John 1:20, 27).

It is apparent that even the followers of John thought that he might be resistant to having his star lose its luster when Jesus' star was on the rise. One of John's disciples raised this very issue: "Rabbi, the man who was with you on the other side of the Jordan—the one you testified about—well, he is baptizing, and *everyone is going to him*" (John 3:26, emphasis added).

John was absolutely secure in himself, for he knew his assigned role: "To this John replied, 'A man can receive only what is given him from heaven. You yourselves can testify that I said, "I am not the Christ, but am sent ahead of him." The bride belongs to the bridegroom. The friend who attends the bridegroom waits and listens for him, and is full of joy when he hears the bridegroom's voice. That joy is mine, and it is now complete. He must become greater; I must become less'" (John 3:27-30). John says that his role is to be the friend of the bridegroom, and the people who go after Jesus are the bride. All he came to do was make the introduction. His job has now come to completion.

John did no less and no more than what he was called to do. When he saw that his work was complete, his joy was full.

The issue for leaders is that of rootedness. Do we know who we are and what motivates us in kingdom work? In his devotional classic *Ordering Your Private World,* Gordon MacDonald powerfully highlights the subtle dangers of losing our way. He contrasts the *called* person with the perils of being a *driven* person. In a nutshell, called people live from the inside out, whereas driven people live from the outside in. Called people order their private world and thereby engage their outer world from a centered existence. Driven people are externally focused because the success standards of this world shape their motivation.

How can you know whether you are driven or called? MacDonald helps us by giving us the symptoms of a *driven* person. The overarching symptom is that driven people are stressed and anxious because there is so much pleasing to do.

Examine your own life against these signs of drivenness:

- *Gratified by accomplishment.* Accumulation of accomplishments is the carrot for which driven people strive. They have learned that they are rewarded for achievement and have come to love the affirmation that comes with it.

- *Gratified by the symbols of accomplishment.* What are the symbols that count in your field of endeavor? Office size? Office window? Position on the organizational chart? Special perks? Salary? House size, luxury and location? Second house? Car model? Vacation opportunities? Charles Colson tells the story of his rise in the Nixon White House in the late 1960s. Having joined the president's legal team a few months after President Nixon came to power, Colson's office was located far down the hallway from the Oval Office. But soon the game of musical offices began, and he found himself next the president's. The press took notice. He was now a man of importance because he was situated next to power. He got the attention and he allowed it to corrupt him.

- *Uncontrolled pursuit of expansion.* Whatever the pursuit, it must be bigger and better, always seeking the next opportunity. Gordon MacDonald quotes the nineteenth-century English preacher Charles Spurgeon: "Success can go to my head and will unless I remember that it is God who accomplishes the work, that he can continue to do so without my help, and that he will be able to make out with other means whenever he wants to cut me out."[1] The need for expansion is a symptom of internal dissatisfaction. Enough is never enough. The pressure is not only on yourself but often evidences itself in being displeased with peers and subordinates, who are instruments of your desire for expansion.

- *Limited regard for integrity.* When our worldly ambitions outstrip the development of our hearts, an integrity gap results. The values that we thought we held dear can readily be compromised. Deceit sets in, and we are its first victim. This truth is portrayed daily as corporate executives and political leaders are shamefully jailed, having violated, by their own admission, standards they once valued. The moral compass has lost its directional arm.

- *Limited or undeveloped people skills.* Driven people focus on goals, objectives and tasks, and often see people as simply one of the tools or resources necessary to get there. There is particular danger here for a visionary. What starts out as God's vision turns into a get-there-at-all costs attitude! Often the cost is a trail of bodies and a revolving door of employees, used and discarded. One of my favorite dark-humor websites is *despair.com*. One of the slides, which pictures the pyramids of Egypt, is titled "Achievement." The caption reads, "You can do anything you set your mind to when you have vision, determination and an endless supply of expendable labor." It is a sad truth that many Christian organizations are run by people who destroy other people in the process because "they get the job done."

- *Volcanic anger.* Anger is just an extension of limited or undeveloped people skills. If people are tools that are not fulfilling their desired function, then get rid of them and get another tool. People who appear to thwart the goals of the leader face the leader's wrath because they are impeding progress.
- *Abnormally busy.* As much as some leaders may complain about and seek pity for their overbooked schedules, they wouldn't take a way out if it was offered. There is something in them that equates busyness with importance, thus busyness is worn as a badge of honor.

In contrast to drivenness, John the Baptist showed a remarkable capacity to live within the confines of his prescribed role. He accomplished only what God had called him to. Instead of unlimited expansion, he remained true to his role as forerunner and was not tempted by the suggestion that he was the Messiah. His integrity was always intact because he kept himself focused on the one who

would come after him and who was greater than he. And though he expressed anger, it was toward the sin that separated people from the holy God.

A word about ambition. Both the *driven* and the *called* demonstrate ambition. Ambition is a God-given quality. Ambition is simply the desire to succeed or to strive for excellence and impact. Driven people are ambitious to obtain worldly acclaim. Those with a call are ambitious to advance God's glory. They live for an audience of One. John R. Mott, probably the greatest evangelist and Christian statesman of the nineteenth century, had his life completely turned around with three short sentences: "Young man, seekest thou great things for thyself? Seek them not. Seek ye first the kingdom of God."

SECOND LESSON

John the Baptist did not allow his ego to be in competition with Jesus. John's role was to be the set-up man for Jesus. He didn't allow his temporary popularity to create a false sense of self-importance. When Jesus came on the scene, John's opinion of himself never got in the way.

There is a remarkable scene that unfolds in John 1. The day after John has explained to the religious leaders that he is not the Christ, and that he awaits someone whose sandals he is not worthy to untie, John sees Jesus coming toward him. John immediately recognizes Jesus because the Spirit, in the form of a dove, has alighted upon Jesus. So he exclaims, "Look, the Lamb of God who takes away the sin of the world! This is the one I meant when I said, 'A man who comes after me has surpassed me because he was before me' " (John 1:29-31). The very next day John is with two of his disciples when he again cries out, "Look, the

Lamb of God!" (John 1:35). The two disciples immediately leave John and follow Jesus.

What is remarkable is that John was not only able to let his disciples go, but he had prepared them to follow another. As those who were formerly in his fold began to drift toward Jesus, John could have felt his life was draining away. But there was no tug of war. This is the mark of true humility.

The opposite of humility is pride and possession. These impulses get us into trouble because we subtly become the focus. Humility and self-conceit are direct opposites. C. S. Lewis calls pride "the complete anti-God state of mind."[2]

We can tell that pride lurks within when we are snubbed, passed over or not recognized for our accomplishments. In such situations we might subtly ask, "Do you know who I am?" The very nature of pride is that it can't remain quiet; it seeks recognition. A personal confession: I (Greg) was attending a church conference and became aware within myself of the conceit of hoping people might recognize my name. After all, I am a published author and am known in certain circles. Oh, how our sense of worth is rooted in the need for others to tell us how valuable we are! I had to ask myself, *Could I be lost in anonymity and be fine with that because my worth is established as a beloved child of the Father?* Only when we are firmly grounded in Christ's pleasure in us, not needing the strokes of the crowd, are we free to be

"IT IS A LAW OF LIFE THAT WE CONSISTENTLY UNDERVALUE THE SIZE OF OUR OWN FAULTS AND OVERVALUE THE SIZE OF OTHERS'. WE ALL HAVE A CRITICAL VALUE OF JUDGING IN OUR OWN FAVOR."

Frederick Dale Brunner, *Matthew: A Commentary, The Christbook, Matthew 1—12*

the leader God intended.

There is a distressing pattern in Christian leadership today. Too many leaders have a grandiose view of themselves, which shows in their narcissism. *Grandiosity* means having an inflated sense of one's importance. A *narcissist* is infatuated with the reflection of his or her own image. This is a sick self-love. Narcissists allow no one else to share the spotlight, because their ego must have no rivals.

I raise this issue because the Christian community seems to reflect the world's desire to have leaders who are driven, because we can then draft off their charismatic personalities. We would rather borrow from other people's energy and be taken along by them than be plugged into the energy of the Holy Spirit ourselves. Since people tend to be passive spectators, the church is particularly vulnerable to narcissistic leaders. The typical Christian is perfectly happy to watch a self-absorbed performer.

C. S. Lewis was very aware of this tendency in himself. Walter Hooper once asked Lewis if he was aware that, regardless of his intentions, Lewis was "winning worship" because of the popularity of his books. Hooper reports that in a still, low voice, and the most complete humility he had ever observed, Lewis replied, "One cannot be too careful not to think of it."[3]

John the Baptist had settled the deeper issue of who he was living for. He knew the role he had been given and that his value came from the Father who assigned his part. Since

John's identity wasn't rooted in popular recognition, he didn't need to compete with Jesus to be the leading man.

LESSON THREE

John the Baptist was suspicious of nothing more than his own soul. Though John had a very special role as the appointed forerunner to the Messiah, he was a sinner like everyone else. The baptism of repentance that he administered was as much for himself as for the "brood of vipers" that needed to flee the wrath to come. When Jesus presented himself to John to be baptized, John recoiled at the thought. "I need to be baptized by you, and do you come to me?" (Matthew 3:14). In the presence of the sinless One, John knew that the roles should be reversed.

Humble leaders know that they are made with feet of clay and therefore must keep a vigilant watch over the inclination of their own souls. The subtle and insidious *drive* that seeks external rewards and the *pride* that expresses itself in competition are directly at odds with the humility that makes us useful as leaders in God's kingdom.

Jonathan Edwards perhaps had the finest theological mind *and* passionate heart that America has ever produced. Edwards was both

> "BOASTING IS THE RESPONSE OF PRIDE TO SUCCESS. SELF-PITY IS THE RESPONSE OF PRIDE TO SUFFERING. BOASTING SAYS, "I DESERVE ADMIRATION BECAUSE I HAVE ACHIEVED SO MUCH." SELF-PITY SAYS, "I DESERVE ADMIRATION BECAUSE I HAVE SACRIFICED SO MUCH." BOASTING IS THE VOICE OF PRIDE IN THE HEART OF THE STRONG. SELF-PITY IS THE VOICE OF PRIDE IN THE HEART OF THE SELF-SACRIFICING."
>
> John Piper, *Desiring God*

a participant in and a careful pastor over the era known as the First Great Awakening (1720s-1740s). Even as a revival was well underway, Edwards warned that spiritual pride was the greatest enemy of the Lord's renewing work. He teaches us how to avoid pride and gives us wonderful insight into spiritual humility. "The spiritually proud person is preoccupied with the state of the spiritual health of others. Seeing themselves as having arrived spiritually, they are quick to find fault, and look upon others as not having nearly the same zeal as they do. Whereas the humble person recognizes that they have so far to go themselves, that they are not apt to be 'busy with other hearts.' "[4]

Edward's insights into spiritual humility serve as the foundation for where we need to be. The writer of Proverbs admonishes us, "Above all else, guard your heart, / for it is the wellspring of life" (Proverbs 4:23). In other words, brackish water can just as easily flow from within as clear, refreshing water. Tend to the clarity of your heart. May the warning of the prophet Jeremiah be ever before us, "The heart is deceitful above all things and beyond cure. / Who can understand it?" (Jeremiah 17:9). In other words, we human beings seem to have an almost infinite capacity for self-deception.

How then do we keep watch over our souls to keep us focused on godly humility? Is our own self-examination enough? The evangelical tradition, reinforced by the radical individualism of our Western culture, has tended to promote the personal devotional life or quiet time, as if these were sufficient. The idea is to get alone with God, bring a Bible, perhaps a devotional guide and a prayer journal for reflection. I'm not suggesting that this isn't impor-

tant, it is just not enough. This "me and Jesus" form of the faith can simply add to an already-distorted self-image.

We need others who will help us watch over our souls. Fortunately, today we are rediscovering that the "cure of the soul" requires skillful spiritual surgeons.

A sign that we have truly understood the greasy pole of humility is our desire to seek out others who help us keep our heart pure.

[1]Gordon MacDonald, *Ordering Your Private World* (Nashville: Thomas Nelson, 1985), p. 33.

[2]C. S. Lewis, *Mere Christianity* (New York: Macmillan, 1952), p. 109.

[3]C. S. Lewis, *The Weight of Glory and Other Addresses* (New York: Macmillan, 1949), p. xix.

[4]Jonathan Edwards, "Thoughts on the Revival in New England," in *The Great Awakening,* ed. C. C. Goen (New Haven, Conn.: Yale University Press, 1972), p. 418.

Leadership Exercise: Keep Watch Over Your Heart

Pride is a hidden sin. It operates under the veil of the lack of self-awareness. C. S. Lewis put it this way in *Mere Christianity,* "There is no fault which we are more unconscious of in ourselves. . . . If anyone would like to acquire humility, I can, I think, tell them the first step. The step is to realize that one is proud. And a biggish step, too."

In this leadership exercise, we will take stock of where pride lurks in us as a means of watching over our hearts.

SYMPTOMS OF A DRIVEN PERSONALITY

Review the signs of drivenness in the reading "He Must Increase, I Must Decrease." Which signs are true of you? For every one you check, give a specific example from your life to support it.

____ Driven people are gratified by accomplishment.

____ Driven people are gratified by the symbols of accomplishment.

____ Driven people are caught in the uncontrolled pursuit of expansion.

____ Driven people tend to have a limited regard for integrity.

____ Driven people often possess limited or undeveloped people skills.

____ Driven people often possess a volcanic force of anger.

____ Driven people are abnormally busy.

As you review these signs of drivenness, what conclusions can you draw about yourself?

How might you pursue living more from the inside out rather than the outside in?

THE COMPETITIVENESS OF PRIDE

Humility and pride are often where we find our identity and therefore our worth and value. Competitiveness or comparisons with others may be a sign that our true worth is not yet fully found in Christ's affirmation of us.

The author illustrated from his own life the desire to be recognized at a recent conference. Where might you be aware of a similar need for recognition as a basis for your worth?

SEEKING HELP TO KEEP WATCH OVER YOUR SOUL

It is not enough to keep watch over our souls privately. We need others. We need others to ask the hard questions. We need someone to whom we confess our sin and hear the declaration of forgiveness in Christ. What next step do you need to take to establish a relationship with someone who can help you "keep watch over your soul?"

The following list identifies relationships that can help us to watch over our souls. Which of these seems like the right kind to pursue?

- *Mentor.* A mentor is a person with a serving, giving, encouraging attitude who you believe you can learn from. This person can ask insightful questions of you as well as share out of the wisdom of his or her life experience. This one-to-one relationship is initiated by the person desiring a mentor. Is there someone who comes to mind?

- *Spiritual friend or accountability partner.* A spiritual friend or accountability partner is a person with whom you can reciprocally disclose struggles, failures and temptations. Seek a godly friend who is committed to asking the hard questions, who is willing to challenge you and is given to encouragement and prayer. In this relationship, it's important to be able to get to the point of being nakedly confessional and receiving a word of forgiveness. Is there someone who is willing to go there with you?

- *Spiritual guide or director.* A spiritual guide or director is usually someone who has received certified training in spiritual direction. Spiritual directors can be found at retreat centers, on church staffs and increasingly among trained lay leaders. The use of the title "director" is somewhat of a misnomer, for it implies a much more directive role than is actually the case. A spiritual director actually is more of a discerning presence, helping a person to see how God is at work in the desires of the individual's heart and assisting him or her to be released to those desires.

- *Covenant or accountability group.* Covenant or accountability groups are generally comprised of three to five people, usually of the same gender, who act as a corporate spiritual friend. Group agendas can consist of sharing spiritual journeys, logging in on temptations and pitfalls, prayerfully interceding for the Holy Spirit's power to fuel the heart and the like. The frequency of meetings varies according to the availability and proximity of the participants.

- *Other.* _____

Which option seems right for you? What step will you take?

Going Deeper

MacDonald, Gordon. *Ordering Your Private World.* Nashville: Thomas Nelson, 1985.

Lewis, C. S. "Pride," *Mere Christianity.* New York: Macmillan, 1952.

Part Two

The Posture of a Leader

What do we mean by *posture?* Well, this unit is not about proper etiquette per se, but, as you will see, it is not unrelated. Posture is the way we carry or position our bodies, and leadership includes how we deport or position ourselves with those we are called to lead. Effective leadership by the world's standards is often measured simply against the bottom line: She got the job done. In business, this usually means satisfying the shareholders with an ever-increasing rate of return on their stock portfolio. In politics the object is to get elected and reelected, which means remaining popular with one's constituents.

Yet Christian leadership is just as concerned about the *means* as it is about the *ends*. In other words, the manner in which one leads is as vital as what is accomplished. For example, funds for a project may have been raised successfully, but the way it was done may have done considerable damage to relationships, creating schism. By biblical standards, schism means that leadership has missed the mark. A leader might intimidate or bully others to comply with their wishes, creating a reign of fear. A board of directors may put up with this because the leader is "effective." But this cannot be considered Christian behavior.

Therefore in part two, we will study three ways Christian leaders position themselves before those they lead.

Kneeling (chap. 4). Servant leadership is an overused and a mostly misunderstood term. So in chapter four we attempt to show that servant leadership does not mean non-leadership. Leadership is the effective of use of power and influence to move people to accomplish a common goal. Christian leadership has to do with how power and influence reflect the One who is our quintessential model of servanthood. Jesus knelt before his disciples as he washed their grimy feet. This act became a visual example for their future behavior. This chapter addresses how servant leaders empower their followers so that all can make a contribution.

Teaming (chap. 5). The New Testament model of leadership is neither John Wayne nor the Lone Ranger charging into conflict. More appropriately, Christian leadership is less about Moses coming down from Mount Sinai having consulted with God and more about becoming a team where all the members' gifts are marshaled to accomplish a mission.

New Testament leaders, though visionaries, understand that God works primarily through the body of Christ. Just as our triune God is an eternal, loving community of Father, Son and Holy Spirit, this reality is to be lived out in the community called the church. It should give a leader no greater pleasure than to see others flourishing as fellows ministers.

Stewarding (chap. 6). Leaders make their greatest contributions when they are true to the way God has designed them. Just as leaders want to see the members of the team functioning and contributing in accord with their God-given talents, gifts, personality and passions, the same should be true for themselves. It isn't selfish for Christian leaders to want to serve the way they are best wired. The communities that the leaders serve would be wise to help their leaders be good stewards of the purpose for which they were made. Chapter six will assist leaders to zero in on the uniqueness of their contribution to building the kingdom of God.

4 / Kneeling

LOOKING AHEAD

Memory Verse: Mark 10:42-45
Bible Study: John 13:1-17
Reading: What Is Servant Leadership?
Leadership Exercise: Taking Stock of the Why and How of Our Leadership

 Core Truth

What is the motivation and posture of a Christian leader?

Leading disciples are not motivated by the self-aggrandizement of control or power, nor by the need to fill a deficit of self-worth. A servant leader finds joy in empowering and equipping others so they can experience the fulfillment of their God-given contribution. The freedom to be a servant leader comes from the reality of being a beloved child of the Father.

1. Identify key words or phrases in the question and answer above, and state their meaning in your own words.

2. Restate the core truth in your own words.

3. What questions or issues does the core truth raise for you?

> "GOD IS MORE PLEASED WITH CERTAIN ACTIONS, HOWEVER FEW THEY MAY BE, DONE IN SILENCE AND IN SECRET, AND WITHOUT DESIRE THAT MEN MIGHT SEE THEM, THAN WITH A THOUSAND GRAND ACTIONS UNDERTAKEN WITH THE INTENTION OF THEIR BECOMING KNOWN TO MEN."
>
> John of the Cross, *Three Mystics*

Memory Verse Study Guide

Copy the entire text here:

Memory Verse: Mark 10:42-45

Often the most influential life lessons occur when we are caught up short. Jesus did some of his best teaching in the real-life settings at hand, offering a word of correction and contrast. In Mark 10:42-45 James and John's desire for greatness provides Jesus the opportunity to redefine leadership according kingdom values.

1. *Putting it in context.* In Mark 10:35-45 Jesus presents a model of leadership that contrasts with the world's prevailing standard. What is the world's standard, and how had James and John bought into it?

2. What evidence do you see in the world or the church of a "lording it over them" / "exercising authority over them" approach to leadership?

3. Jesus clearly is calling those who lead in his kingdom to a different way. Put in your own words what greatness (or being first) looks like in God's kingdom.

4. If someone were to say to you "To be a *servant* or *slave* means always being ready to respond to the expressed needs of others," would you agree or disagree? Explain your response.

5. In verse 45, what does Jesus' willingness to serve by giving his life as a ransom for many teach us about our relationship with those we lead?

Inductive Bible Study Guide

Bible Study: John 13:1-17

On the eve of his crucifixion, Jesus demonstrates servant love to his disciples. None of them had been willing to assume the posture of a household slave and wash the others' feet. We know that even at this juncture as they gathered for the Passover meal, the disciples were still debating among themselves who was the greatest (Luke 22:24).

1. Read John 13:1-17. Put in your own words the dramatic moment at which Jesus and the disciples had arrived (vv. 1-2).

2. How does verse 3 serve as the foundation for Jesus' freedom to serve his disciples?

What does this tell us about what we need to know in order to be a servant?

"SPIRITUAL ABUSE ON THE PART OF A SPIRITUAL LEADER RESULTS WHENEVER SPIRITUAL MENTORING, TEACHING, AND GUIDANCE IS USED TO GAIN CONTROL AND REINFORCE THE AUTHORITY OF THE LEADER RATHER THAN TO EMPOWER AND NURTURE THE ONES LED."

Ray Anderson, *The Soul of Ministry*

3. What is the symbolic significance of the foot washing? What might be a present-day equivalent?

4. Why do you suppose Peter vehemently resisted Jesus' attempt to wash his feet (v. 8)?

5. What is the correlation between our willingness to be served and our ability to serve others?

6. What did Jesus want his disciples to learn from having their feet washed (vv. 12-15)?

7. Connect leadership and servanthood. How does one inform the other?

8. What questions or issues does this passage raise for you?

Reading: What Is Servant Leadership?

The truth is that the term *servant leadership* is often heard as "nonleadership." Practically speaking, the modifier *servant* seems to cancel out *leadership:* the leader assumes the posture of servant, which means to be at the beck and call of others. In an article titled "What It Means to Be a Pastor," one pastor captured his understanding of *servant leadership:* "Even though I may disappoint you at times, you may expect of me service. I am Christ's servant. Therefore, I am also your servant. When, you may ask, is the right time to call upon your servant? In the morning when I am well-rested? At a more convenient time in my busy schedule? After more important matters of church policy and administration are considered? No. The right time is when you have a need."[1]

As noble a portrait of a servant as this may first appear, it conjures the image of a butler whose ears are tuned to the whims of his master's bell. Is this what we mean by servant leadership? No.

Aubrey Malphurs offers this alternative definition of servant leadership: "A Christian leader is a godly person (character) who knows where he is going (vision) and has followers (influence)."[2] In other words, a leader leads. A leader must have (1) a picture of a preferred future, and (2) the ability to influence people to embrace that future. Yet for leadership to be Christian it must follow the example of our Master, who is the essence of a servant leader. *Servant* qualifies the approach to leadership by addressing the why (motives) and the how (style).

Leadership exercises power and influence toward a God-inspired vision. The main question of servant leadership is, *How are power and influence exercised, and in what spirit?* These are the issues that Jesus addressed head-on in his encounter with James and John. These sons of Zebedee were mired in the prevailing understanding of leadership.

James and John approached Jesus on the sly to put in their bid for a place of privilege in Jesus' future kingdom. Jesus had promised that when he ascended to his glorious throne, the twelve disciples would occupy thrones as judges over the tribes of Israel (Matthew 19:28). Hearing this, James and John decided to establish the seating arrangements in the throne room. So they asked Jesus, "Let one of us sit at your right and the other at your left in your glory" (Mark 10:37).

The word spread quickly that these two had attempted an end run around the other ten. The others were irate. "When the ten heard about this, they became indignant with James and John" (Mark 10:41). We might assume that Peter led the offended delegation to Jesus, since the brothers had broken ranks with the favored triad made up of Peter, James and John. The ten weren't upset because James and John had misunderstood the nature of kingdom leadership, but because they (the ten) were beaten to the punch.

Jesus saw this as a teachable moment. He contrasted the world's understanding of leadership, power and influence to his understanding of the *why* and *how* of leadership. "Jesus called them together and said, 'You know that those who are regarded as rulers of the Gentiles lord it over them, and their high officials exercise authority over them'" (Mark 10:42). Jesus recognized the disciples' same desire for power that he saw in the Roman and Jewish authorities. The dominant paradigm is captured in the phrases "lord it *over* them" and "exercise authority *over* them." Leadership is equated with dominance—"over them."

James and John were ambitious, striving for greatness. There is nothing wrong with that. But their motivation was wrong. James and John seem to be misguided in two ways.

Honor. James and John sought to build their sense of worth and value by their closeness to the center of power. They could bask in reflected glory by being in the favored position, nearest the throne. Their inward deficit could be masked because they had "arrived"; they had risen to the top. Now, many would pay deference them. Of course, the doors of privilege would open at their command because power gets what it wants. What a drug this is.

Every profession has its hierarchy of status. In business, status comes in the form of people knowing your name, being waited on by an administrative assistant, having a comfortable environment, getting the best table at a restaurant. If you want an earful, ask a nurse about the pecking order in the medical field. But the academic world may be the most stratified of all with its degrees, titles, honors, faculty dining rooms and so on.

The gravitational pull of status surrounds us. It's so subtle we're often not conscious of its effect. But it most certainly has a hold on us.

The following poem by Robert Raines raises the issue of whether our relationships are calculated to help us better our position.

I am like James and John,
Lord, I size up other people
    in terms of what they can do for me;
    how they can further my program,

    feed my ego,
    satisfy my needs,
    give me strategic advantage.
I exploit people,
    ostensibly for your sake,
    but really for my own sake. . . .
I am like James and John.[3]

Power. If honor is our measure of worth in relation to the standard above us, then power has to do with our comparative position over those below us. Pride can be defined as power used to enhance our ego. What were James and John up to in their secretive request? They wanted to be exalted over the other ten. C. S. Lewis reminds us that at its essence pride is competitive. Lewis writes:

> Pride gets no pleasure out of having something, only out of having more of it than the next man. We say that people are proud of being rich, or clever, or good-looking, but they are not. They are proud of being richer, or cleverer, or better-looking than others. . . . It is the comparison that makes you proud: the pleasure of being above the rest.[4]

Jim Collins has written a fascinating study on what makes for a great company in his very successful business book *Good to Great*. Great companies, he asserts, are led by "Level 5" leaders. Though Collins's reference point is not the biblical paradigm of servant leadership, his description of Level 5 leaders closely resembles the kind of servant leaders Jesus is calling his followers to be. Collins says that Level 5 leaders display a duality of modesty and willingness, humility and fearlessness.

We will come back to this profile in a moment, but what is of interest at this point is Collins's discussion of "Level 4" leaders. Level 4 leaders seem to fit the picture of what James and John aspired to be. They are concerned with their own personal greatness. Their focus is not the long-term success of the company but that they are acknowledged as the reason for the success now. "After all, what better testament to your own personal greatness than that the place falls apart after you leave."[5] The favorite subject of ego-driven leaders is themselves, and they love to hog the spotlight. In an article by a Level 4 leader on leading change, the author used the pronoun *I* forty-four times and *we* sixteen times. Collins concluded, "In over two thirds of the comparison cases [i.e., of leaders of good but not great companies], we noted the presence of a gargantuan personal ego that contributed to the demise or continued mediocrity of the company."[6]

Jesus' approach to leadership was diametrically opposed to seeking honor and deriving value through pursuing the world's perks while exercising authority as an ego-enhancing endeavor. "Not so with you. Instead, whoever wants to become great among you must be your servant, and whoever wants to be first must be slave of all. For even the Son of Man did not come to be served, but to serve, and give his life as a ransom for many" (Mark 10:43-45).

> "AT ONE FELL SWOOP, JESUS UNEQUIVOCALLY REJECTED THE HIERARCHICAL MODEL AS THE BASIS FOR COMMUNAL ORGANIZATION AMONG CHRISTIANS AND REPLACED IT WITH AN ALTERNATIVE CONTRAST MODEL OF DOWNWARD MOBILITY, PATTERNED ON HIS OWN ITINERARY OF HUMILIATION FROM THE HIGHEST GLORY TO THE LOWEST CONDITION AS CRUCIFIED SAVIOR."
>
> Gilbert Bilezikian, *Community 101*

Let's draw out the implications of servant leadership using the categories of *why* and *how*.

WHY? SO THAT OTHERS MAY FIND LIFE

Servant leaders are not concerned with receiving praise. President Harry Truman is attributed with the saying: "You can accomplish anything in life, provided you do not mind who gets the credit."[7] Servant leaders are concerned with two things: (1) that God's dream for the people they lead becomes a reality, and (2) that all involved feel valued for the contribution they make to the fulfillment of the vision.

Let's return to the profile of the Level 5 leader. The profile of the great leader is not one that Collins's team set out to prove, but one that emerged as they saw what great companies had in common. First, Level 5 leaders are not household names. In fact, unless you are in the same industry, the chances of recognizing any of them would be remote. Second, Level 5 leaders don't like to talk about themselves; instead, they focus on the company and the contributions of others. The following terms describe a Level 5 leader: quiet, humble, modest, reserved, shy, gracious, mild-mannered, self-effacing and understated; they do not believe their own press clippings. "The good-to-great leaders never wanted to become larger-than-life heroes. They never aspired to be put on a pedestal or become unreachable icons. They were seemingly ordinary people quietly producing extra-ordinary results."[8]

Since there are many people who have these qualities, what set these particular people apart as leaders? First, they were absolutely focused on the success of the corporate enterprise and not their own personal aggrandizement. Second, they had a ferocious determination to do whatever it would take to make the company great. In other words, being a leader wasn't about themselves but something bigger. When asked about their success, they tend to credit the great team that had formed around them (or other external factors). In answer to the question, Why don't we have more Level 5 leaders? Collins says there are "people who could never in a million years bring themselves to subjugate their egoistic needs to the greater ambition of building something larger and more lasting than themselves. For these people, work will always be first and foremost about what they get—fame, fortune, adulation, power, whatever—not what they build, create, and contribute."[9]

Servant leaders are willing to give their lives that God's vision for his people becomes a reality. Jesus set the pace here: "For even the Son of Man did not come to be served, but to serve, and to give his life as a ransom for many" (Mark 10:45). What we notice about the great servant leaders is that they have such a deep love for and identification with the people they serve that they are willing figuratively to give their own life on behalf of the people.

Moses demonstrated servant leadership when God was ready to judge the Hebrews for their idolatry (bowing before the golden calf). Moses said to God, "But now, please forgive their sin—but if not, blot me out of the book you have written" (Exodus 32:32). The apostle Paul echoed a similar sentiment in writing to the Romans: "I have great sorrow and unceasing anguish in my heart. For I could wish that I myself were cursed and cut off from Christ for the sake of my brothers, those of my own race, the people of Israel" (Romans 9:2-4).

Jesus, Moses and Paul demonstrate the kind of love for the people of God that a parent has for a terminally ill child. If our child had kidney failure and could be saved by donating one of our own kidneys, we would not hesitate to make that sacrifice. Why? The child's welfare is even more important than our own. The wandering and clueless people of Israel led Jesus to tears; he cried out "how often I have longed to gather your children together, as a hen gathers her chicks under her wings, but you were not willing" (Matthew 23:37). And though the people of Israel had been disobedient and recalcitrant, Moses

> "NO MAN IS SECURE IN HIGH POSITION SAVE HE WHO WOULD GLADLY BE SUBJECT. NO MAN CAN FIRMLY COMMAND SAVE HE WHO HAS LEARNED GLADLY TO OBEY. NO MAN SPEAKS SURELY SAVE HE WHO WOULD GLADLY KEEP SILENCE IF HE MIGHT."
>
> Thomas á Kempis, *The Imitation of Christ*

longed to see them in the Promised Land. And even though Paul was called to serve the Gentiles, his heart remained with Israel. Servant leaders find themselves anguishing in prayer over those who have yet to fully appreciate all that God has for them.

HOW: BRINGING OUT THE BEST IN OTHERS

Servant leaders are an example of what others can become. Servant leaders empower others through modeling. They motivate others by their own example. Instead of driving people through overbearing authority, servant leaders draw them through an attractive life. Again Jesus is the pacesetter. On the eve of his crucifixion Jesus gathered with his disciples to celebrate Passover in the upper room. While the disciples debated who was greatest among them (Luke 22:24), Jesus wrapped a towel around his waist and knelt before each of them with washbasin in hand. He played the role of a common household slave, washing the grimy, dust-caked feet of his followers. This action said more than any verbal instruction could have. But so they would not miss the import of his action, he explained: "Do you understand what I have done for you?" . . . "You call me 'Teacher' and 'Lord', and rightly so, for that is what I am. Now that I, your Lord and Teacher, have washed your feet, you also should wash one another's feet. I have set you an example that you should do as I have done for you" (John 13:12-15).

The sobering truth is that our life speaks

> "IF A PERSON SAYS HE IS A LEADER AND NO ONE IS FOLLOWING, THEN HE IS NOT A LEADER. AS SOMEONE HAS SAID, 'HE IS SIMPLY TAKING A WALK.'"
>
> Aubrey Malphurs, *Pouring New Wine into Old Wineskins*

more loudly than our words. People are either drawn to us because of what they see or they are repelled because our life contradicts what we say. Would we want to invite others to live as we are living? Bill Hybels, the founding pastor at Willow Creek Community Church, put it this way: When we are inviting others to follow Jesus Christ, we must remember that we are asking them to either trade up or to trade down. Is life in Christ so rich for us that we can say, "Give up your current life for the one I am living in Christ"? Servant leadership is rooted in example.

Servant leaders are committed to bringing out the best in others through empowering them. Truly great athletes are said to make everyone around them better players. In basketball a good point guard is able to get everyone on the team involved. Servant leaders find joy in working with a team to accomplish something that no one team member could do alone. Remember, when asked about their success Level 5 leaders speak about the contributions of others and not about themselves. The fundamental role of church leaders, according to the apostle Paul, is to bring the members of the body of Christ to their fullness. Servant leaders are "to prepare God's people for works of service, so that the body of Christ may be built up" (Ephesians 4:12).

Servant leaders find their greatest joy in seeing others fulfill the vision that God has for their lives. There is nothing that touches a servant leader more than the testimony of someone who, under the guidance of the leader, has gone from surviving to thriving, experiencing a God-given potential that he or she did not even know was there.

What are the results of your leadership? What will people say? Will there be stories praising how much *you* did? Or will the conversation center around what the *team* did together, and how good the members felt about their contribution to the mission? An old Chinese saying captures this well, "The wicked leader is hated by the people; the good leader is revered by the people; the great leader is when the people said, 'We did it ourselves.'" The measure of your leadership is not just what is accomplished when you are present but what is sustained when you aren't around. Great leaders empower their people to accomplish great things in their absence.

BELOVED OF THE FATHER

In conclusion, servant leadership is qualified by godly impulse (why), and it motivates by example and empowerment (how). But what will allow us to sublimate our ego and take up the posture of a servant? How might we be released from the need to control so others can be themselves? How can our leadership be exercised in a way that we are not seeking love but are able to freely give it? The answer: *we*

must know that we are a beloved child of God.

Why was Jesus free to be the servant of all? John introduces Jesus' humble service to his disciples with these words. "Jesus knew that the Father had put all things under his power, and that he had come from God and was returning to God; so he go up from the meal, took off his outer clothing, and wrapped a towel around his waist" (John 13:3-4). Jesus was a servant to the disciples because his value was firmly established by his Father.

We will only be free to be a servant leader when deep in our identity we know that we are a beloved child of the Father. Jesus ministry began and ended with this knowledge. If our leadership is an attempt to make up for missing value or to fill a deficit, then servant leadership will elude us. Brennan Manning tells the story of an Irish priest taking a walk in his rural parish. He comes across an old peasant kneeling in prayer by the side of the road. Impressed, the priest said, "You must be very close to God." The peasant raised his head and smiled, "Yes, He's very fond of me." Our ability to be a servant will grow in direct proportion to our ability to hear for ourselves, "This is my [child], chosen and marked by my love, the pride of my life" (Matthew 3:17 *The Message*).

---

[1]Sherman Roddy, "What It Means to Be a Pastor," *Leadership Journal* (Winter 1990).
[2]Aubrey Malphurs, *Pouring New Wine into Old Wineskins* (Grand Rapids: Baker, 1993), p. 163.
[3]Robert Raines, in *Creative Broodings* (New York: Macmillan, 1966).
[4]C. S. Lewis, *Mere Christianity* (New York: Macmillan, 1943), pp. 109-10.
[5]Jim Collins, *Good to Great* (New York: HarperCollins, 2001), p. 26.
[6]Ibid., p. 29.
[7]Harry Truman, quoted in David McCullough, *Truman* (New York: Simon & Schuster, 1992), p. 654.
[8]Collins, *Good to Great,* p. 28.
[9]Ibid., p. 36.

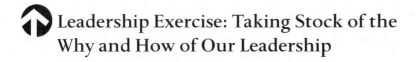

Leadership Exercise: Taking Stock of the Why and How of Our Leadership

Jesus calls us to do the hard work of self-examination. Servant leaders replace worldly motives ("Not so with you") with motives rooted in a servant's heart.

THE MARKS OF A WORLDLY LEADER

Honor. Seeking to be near the center of power and influence as the way to establish worth.

1. In your chosen field of work, what are the marks that you have "made" it?

2. On a scale of 1-5, assess how strongly do these marks motivate you (1 = no appeal; 5 = compelling). Explain.

Power. Seeking to enhance my influence for the sake of my reputation.

3. If you were to monitor your own use of *I* and *we* for a week, which of these do you think you use more? What do you think this says about your self-importance?

THE SERVANT LEADER'S MOTIVE: THAT OTHERS MAY FIND LIFE

4. Servant leaders view people as precious to the heart of God; and the spiritual welfare of people is their own heart burden.

   How would you assess your willingness to carry in your heart the spiritual welfare of the people you serve?

THE SERVANT LEADER'S PRACTICE (HOW): BRINGING OUT THE BEST IN OTHERS

5. Do you think others perceive that you are deeply concerned to know and appreciate the uniqueness of the people on your team? Explain.

6. Think of a particular team you are serving. Write down the names of the people on that team
   and next to them list the gifts, qualities and attributes you believe they bring to the team. Then,
   take the time to affirm them by writing a note, sending an e-mail, using team time to express
   your appreciation of them and so forth.

BELOVED OF THE FATHER

7. Since the ability to be a servant leader is directly proportionate to our sense of security in the
   Father's love, how would your assess your sense of how this reality shapes your identity?
   (Choose one of the following statements that best characterizes where you are at.)

   ___ I'm not sure what this means.

   ___ I'm stuck and can't see how to get there.

   ___ I'm seeking to move this truth from head to heart.

   ___ I want to know more of what this is like.

   ___ I'm beginning to appreciate who I am as God's beloved.

   ___ I have had major breakthroughs in understanding.

   ___ I have always felt deeply valued by God.

Explain:

Going Deeper

Jim Collins. *Good to Great.* New York: Harper Collins, 2004.
Max DePree. *Leadership Is an Art.* New York: Dell Publishing, 1989.

5 / Teaming

LOOKING AHEAD

Memory Verse: 1 Corinthians 12:4-7
Bible Study: Acts 15:1-35
Reading: Team Building: A Practice That Fosters the Ministry of All
Leadership Exercise: Developing a Ministry Team Covenant

 Core Truth

From what do Christian leaders derive their greatest satisfaction?

Leading disciples find their greatest satisfaction when they are used by God to empower a group of people (large or small) to achieve a mission that advances God's kingdom. There is great reward in knowing that all the group members sense the value of the mission, are making a contribution based on the use of their gifts, and are accomplishing more together than they could alone.

1. Identify key words or phrases in the question and answer above, and state their meaning in your own words.

2. Restate the core truth in your own words.

3. What questions or issues does the core truth raise for you?

Memory Verse Study Guide

Copy the entire text here:

Memory Verse: 1 Corinthians 12:4-7

There is no better New Testament image for *team* than the body of Christ. In 1 Corinthians 12, Paul captures the balance between unity and diversity. He celebrates the multiplicity of gifts that are given to all the members of the body who then contribute them to building the unity of the church to accomplish its mission.

1. *Putting it in context.* Read all of 1 Corinthians 12. According to Paul, how should the church function at its best?

2. In verses 4-6, Paul seems to be giving us a glossary of interchangeable terms for spiritual gifts. Each provides its own nuance of meaning. What aspects of spiritual gifts does each term bring out?
   a. gifts (v. 4)
   b. service (v. 5)
   c. working (v. 6)

3. With each of the ways Paul describes the gifts, he also gives us the source. What picture of God does Paul paint? How does the nature of God illustrate unity and diversity?

4. To what end are the gifts to be used (v. 7)?

5. In your experience, how might the gifts of the Spirit be misused in the body of Christ?

6. When have you most felt like you used your gifts to contribute to the accomplishment of a mission?

Inductive Bible Study Guide

Bible Study: Acts 15:1-35

In Acts 15, we come to a crucial point in the early church's decision about the nature of the gospel message. As we consider team ministry, this chapter serves as a case study on how the church worked together to discern God's truth regarding what it means to live under grace.

1. *Read Acts 15:1-5.* How would you state the problem that needed to be resolved by the elders and apostles? What two positions were at odds with each other?

2. How did those who represented both sides believe that their differences could be resolved? What conclusions might you draw from this?

3. *Read Acts 15:6-12.* What was the apostles and elders' approach to how they went about discerning God's truth?

4. *Read Acts 15:13-21.* James, the brother of Jesus, is the appointed spokesperson for the apostles and elders. On what was his decision based? What was that decision?

5. *Read Acts 15:22-35.* How did the apostles and elders go about communicating their decision?

6. As you review this case study, what contributed to making this a peaceable and model decision? What principles of community and team-building might we derive from the process used in the early church?

7. What questions or issues does this passage raise for you?

Reading: Team Building: A Practice That Fosters the Ministry of All

A most fulfilling role for leaders, whether on a macro level (across an organization or church) or micro level (in a small group or team), is creating an environment in which all contribute their God-given gifts to the ministry. This is teamwork.

The greatest satisfaction I (Greg) have had in ministry has come from marshaling the contributions of others toward completing a mission that none of us could have accomplished on our own. It is at these times that the whole is truly greater than the sum of it parts; all involved sense they have added value to the process. A team forms when individuals are synchronized like rowers pulling together to reach the finish line. We experience being the body of Christ when the many members become one (1 Corinthians 12:12). The fundamental biblical paradigm for a team is God as Trinity.

> "TEAM MINISTRY IS OWNERSHIP AND SELF-INITIATED VISION IN WHICH MEMBERS CARRY OUT PLANS THEY THEMSELVES HAVE CONCEIVED OR HAD A PART IN CONCEPTUALIZING."
>
> Daniel Reeves, *Ministry Advantage*

BIBLICAL VISION OF TEAM MINISTRY

Jesus tells us that integral to the fulfillment of the Great Commission is "baptizing [disciples] in the name of the Father and of the Son and of the Holy Spirit" (Matthew 28:19). Why is baptism in the name of the triune God so central to discipleship? The fundamental basis of all reality is the Creator God, who is a community (or team)—Father, Son and Holy Spirit.

Throughout eternity God has been forever a self-existent Being-in-fellowship, the primal loving community. Our identity as God's image-bearers (Genesis 1:26-27) is fulfilled when our life is infused with the life of the One who created us out of and for love. The Father, Son and Holy Spirit are one, yet each divine person has a distinct role that contributes to the loving fellowship. And the church finds its life and ministry when it reflects the unity and diversity modeled in the Trinity.

In *Leading the Team-Based Church* George Cladis reminds us of the image that seventh-century church father John of Damascus proposed to capture the relationships in the Trinity. The Greek word *perichoresis,* translated "circle dance," is a vivid portrait of the trinitarian God. The component parts of *perichoresis* are *peri* and *choros. Choros* refers a round dance performed at banquets or festive occasions. This is then intensified by the prefix *peri,* which emphasizes the circularity of the holy dance. The *perichoretic* image of the Trinity is that of the three divine persons in a continual circular dance that implies intimacy, equality, unity and love—yet distinction. "The oneness of God is not the oneness of a distinct, self-contained individual; it is the unity of a community of persons who love each other and live together in harmony."[1]

When we think of team, the image of "circle" should immediately come to mind. "In a circle we can all see each other. No one is left out. We are all interconnected. We hold up each other."[2]

Paul's image of the body of Christ as the fundamental identity of the church is derived from this trinitarian reality. In 1 Corinthians 12, unity and diversity, oneness and manyness are the poles that capture the way the body is designed to function. Paul presses the point that ministry in the church is made up of the contribution of all the parts. "Now to each one the manifestation of the Spirit is given for the common good" (1 Corinthians 12:7). When Paul speaks of the distribution of the spiritual gifts for ministry he does so in a trinitarian manner. Different kinds of *gifts* come from the Holy Spirit (1 Corinthians 12:4); different kinds of *service* or *ministry* come from the Lord Jesus (1 Corinthians 12:5); different kinds of *working* (literally "energizings") come from God the Father (1 Corinthians 12:6). Paul's point is that the church finds its life and pattern in its triune source. When the church functions at its optimum, ministry is the sum total of what God is doing through everyone's gifts. A friend named Mike Elder summarized this truth at a conference

> "THE COLLABORATIVE
> TEAM RECOGNIZES THE
> UNIQUE GIFTS OF IT
> MEMBERS AND MAKES
> THOSE MEMBERS SHINE.
> THEY RENDER ONE
> ANOTHER'S WEAKNESSES
> IRRELEVANT TO THE
> CAUSE BECAUSE THEY
> FOCUS INSTEAD ON EACH
> OTHER'S GIFTS AND
> POOL THEM TO MOVE
> TOWARD THE MISSION
> GOD HAS GIVEN THE
> TEAM."
>
> George Cladis, *Leading the Team-Based Church*

for the Saratoga Federated Church with this memorable phrase, "We don't have it all together, but together we have it all." None of us is complete in and of ourselves, not even close. God has designed it so that we need each other.

The joyful role of the team-building leader is assisting everyone in joining the dance by making their God-designated contribution to the whole. This is exactly what Paul has in mind when he says that the role of leaders in the Christian community is "to prepare God's people for works of service so that the body of Christ may be built up" (Ephesians 4:11-12). A generation ago Elton Trueblood, the Quaker lay theologian, proposed that the best modern equivalent for an equipper was player-coach. A coach helps each member of the team find their role and grow to their potential in that position. But being a player-coach is more than giving directions from the sidelines. The player-coach also puts him- or herself in the game as a team member. In a former church where I (Greg) served as senior pastor, the motto was "On This Team Everyone Plays." The leader's most fulfilling role is coming alongside the team members and assisting their growth as they make their contribution to the success of the team. Trueblood wrote, "The idea of the pastor as the equipper is one which is full of promise . . . to watch for undeveloped powers, to draw them out, to bring potency to actuality in human lives—this is a self validating task."[3]

Unfortunately, many of us have abandoned the focus on the ministry of the whole body for a corporate model in which professionals are hired to do ministry for us. The move away from an every-member ministry to a professional clergy or CEO model has been disastrous on two accounts.

First, the more professionalized our ministries have become, the more laypeople have been disenfranchised. Gilbert Bilezikian writes, "Awed by the elitist image of trained specialists [clergy or ministry professional], the average church member shrinks away from involvements or reduces them to marginally supportive roles."[4] Second, pastors or organizational leaders themselves are negatively affected. "The clergy-dominant system of doing church places on pastors the unrealistic burden of acting as if they were universally gifted so as to be able to carry successfully the multitude of responsibilities that constitute the life of local congregations."[5] This institutional model of leadership creates passive spectators out of the majority and places backbreaking expectations on its leaders.

New Testament leadership is always team-based. The New Testament images and language for a transformed leadership is breathtaking. Since the church was birthed out of Judaism, the priesthood was the model at hand. Priests were set apart to represent the people before God and God to the people. Yet, surprisingly, leaders of the local church are never called "priests." The priesthood under the final and ultimate high priest, Jesus Christ, now belongs to all believers. Just as everyone is a minister in the body of Christ so everyone is priest (1 Peter 2:4-9).

"There is no evidence in the New Testament that any early Christian community existed that was under the local leadership of one dominant individual," observes Bilezikian.[6] The leaders of the local church, referred to primarily as "elders" (bishops or pastors), without exception are designated in the plural (Acts 14:23; 15:4, 6; 20:17; 21:18; 1 Timothy 4:14; 5:17; Titus 1; James 5:14; 1 Peter 5:1-4). Throughout the New Testament, church leadership is presented as collective ministry. To the extent that a dominant, larger-than-life individual is exalted over a team, the New Testament view of team ministry has been abandoned.

> "WE PREACH TEAMWORK,
>
> BUT WE IDOLIZE
>
> INDIVIDUALISM."
>
> Jean Lipman-Blumen,
> *Connective Leadership*

THE DISAPPOINTMENT OF MINISTRY STRUCTURES

While the New Testament pictures an every-member ministry of the church, laypeople often are disappointed by the actual ministry systems and structures they encounter. Disappointment arises because of the gap between ministry expectations and reality. If you want to discover how people feel about church work, ask what comes to mind when they hear the word *committee*. You will most likely hear a string of words like *boring, slow, meetings, long, tasks* and so forth. Though there may be some positive associations thrown in, by and large the work of the church is not something that stirs positive passions. Yet committees, boards and meetings are the way the church and parachurch groups accomplish their work.

Why are church committees associated with such disappointment, and how can this point us in a life-giving direction? In my (Greg) experience committees fail for the following reasons:

- *Unequal levels of commitment.* The amount of time people are willing to invest and the roles they are willing to assume vary dramatically. Uneven commitment leads to frustration because people are *unequally yoked* to the task.

- *Not mission-focused.* Most committees are designed to keep the program running as is, with little fine-tuning. They meet on a regular time schedule (e.g., once a month for two hours) which is barely enough time to maintain the present structure. These committees aren't centered around the passionate question, What will it take to fulfill our mission?

- *Oversight and policy.* Frank Tillapaugh sarcastically says that a committee is a group of people who get together who ask two questions: (1) What should we do? (2) Who can we get to do it? In other words, committees talk about ministry, but don't do it. A gulf exists between those who make the decisions and those who implement them.

- *Lack of relationships.* A person can serve on a committee for a considerable period of time and not know, for example, that a fellow committee member's spouse is dying of cancer. Ouch!

- *Position and gifts don't match.* Most committee assignments are made before identifying how a member's spiritual gift could contribute to the task.

- *Lack of heart for ministry.* Do members of the committee have a passion for their particular ministry? Usually, this question is not even asked.

These bulleted items point to what will bring satisfaction to committee members. If *committee* is an expression of the corporate or institutional nature of the church (or ministry), *ministry team* is the organic expression of Christ's body: the one and the many, the leader as player-coach, and team leadership.

Rather than committees, boards or task forces, I (Greg) believe that ministry teams are much more consistent with the biblical vision of ministry.

First, a ministry team is a small group of people (three to twelve members) called together by God. Second, the members of a ministry team mutually covenant to care for one another as they exercise their spiritual gifts to meet a heartfelt need.

Let's examine the component parts to see why ministry teams can be so life-giving.

A small group (context). Church or parachurch ministries most effectively comprise focused small groups or "little platoons." Size matters. In order to maximize contributions, every member of a ministry must feel a part of the team and that he or she has something to offer. When a small group has more than twelve members, individual members begin to

> "IN A CIRCLE WE CAN ALL SEE EACH OTHER. NO ONE IS LEFT OUT. WE ARE ALL INTERCONNECTED. WE HOLD UP EACH OTHER."
>
> George Cladis, *Leading the Team-Based Church*

feel like spectators, believing that they won't be missed if they don't show up. Teams with fewer than three members (and even three is questionable) don't have enough firepower to adequately sustain their ministry. Teams of three to twelve members have the flexibility and mobility to adjust and move forward. This optimum size allows the team to focus on its particular mission without being spread too thin. From a historical perspective, small bands of committed people focused on a common cause have made huge contributions to society (e.g., Jesus and the Twelve; William Wilberforce and Clapham Society; John Wesley and class meetings).

pose and design to fill God's will as best they can discern it. . . . They sense that their work has ultimate meaning, they sense that they are proceeding to do something highly significant."[7]

Care for one another (community). Community is often missing in committee work. To be sustained in ministry, group members need to find deep nourishment in the communal connections shared. Chuck Miller, formerly a youth pastor at Labor Avenue Congregational Church in Pasadena, California, used to say that "we need to be the people of God *before* we do the work of God." I would change one word, "we need to be the people of God *as* we do the

Table 5.1. Contrast Between a Committee and Ministry Team

Committee	Ministry Team
Task-focused	Mission/relationship focused
Meets on a routine time schedule	Does what it takes to accomplish its mission
Roles not clearly defined	Clear roles based on gifts
No covenant	Mutual, written covenant
Authority, policy oversight	Authority and responsibility together

Called together by God to meet a heartfelt need (commission). The organizing principle of a team is the mission or vision it forms around. In other words, passion for the group vision is the basis for participation. What the members care deeply about is a key to discerning a team's mission. Mission is formed around need. What need is the group attempting to address (e.g., hunger, counsel to unwed mothers, middle school youth)? According to George Cladis, "Ministry teams are fueled by a mission God has given them to go and do. They act with pur-

work of God." When we share our lives with, grow to trust and find joy in our partnership on a team, we experience true community that gives joy to our lives and service to Christ. If our team doesn't exhibit the qualities we intend to pass on to others, what is the point in the first place?

Exercise spiritual gifts (contribution). Teamwork happens when all the members are empowered to shape the mission of the team and make their God-ordained contribution. A good friend, Paul Ford,[8] says that teams form around three questions: (1) *Where are you powerful?* In other words, what spiritual gifts (God's power through you) has God graced you to share with the team? (2) *What are your weaknesses?* When we (especially leaders) are up front about our deficiencies, this vulnerability is the invitation to community. Sharing our weaknesses is a statement that we need others in order to be complete. Other group members hear this as an invitation because it shows they are needed. (3) *Who do you need?* When we share our weaknesses, we are implicitly declaring "we don't have it all together; only together do we have it all." Cladis notes, "The collaborative team recognizes the unique gifts of it members and makes those members shine. They render one another's weaknesses irrelevant to the cause because they focus instead on each other's gifts and pool them to move toward the mission God has given the team."[9]

Mutually covenant together. The covenant is the glue that holds a team together. *A covenant is a written mutual agreement between two or more parties that specifies the expectations and commitments in the relationship.* This is often the missing ingredient of a team. A major reason for unequal commitments and the lack of shared mission is that the foundation has not been laid through the team-building process of making a covenant. Adding this one element to the team-building process can wonderfully enhance the quality of a ministry team.

Why is a written covenant important?

- A covenant gives the group a mutual understanding of its mission and determines whether the members are called to accomplish it. It is vital that all team members respond affirmatively to key points of the covenant so that there is a shared understanding. The team leader should avoid striking private deals with individual team members. Uneven commitments undermine the team's effort to accomplish the mission. Generally, the group should not allow exceptions to mutual commitments. For example, I (Greg) was a part of strategic elder group that had covenanted to meet three out of four Tuesdays per month to accomplish our mission. Given the high level of commitment, it was difficult to find people who could or would make this kind of time investment. Bill said he could be available two Tuesdays a month. The team decided that if they made an exception for Bill the team's commitment would be watered down. So they reluctantly turned Bill down.

- *Written* covenants are valuable for a number of reasons. Written agreements allow the members to verify whether what they understood in discussion is actually what they are being asked to commit to. Also since memories are faulty, a written agreement serves as an excellent reminder. Potential new members can read the covenant and ask questions before deciding to commit to the team.

- A primary role of the group leader is helping the group keep the covenant they have agreed to. If team members are departing from the covenant, the leader has a tool to pull people back in line without having to be heavy-handed. A covenant should be reviewed and renewed at regular intervals. At that time each member of the team evaluates how he or she is doing in keeping the covenant commitments.

When teams are working well, all the qualities of Christian leadership will become a reality. *We will fall more in love with Christ and deepen our knowledge and trust in him.* When we follow our heart in ministry we find ourselves at the intersection of being and doing. We have tapped into our God-given purpose, which is finding expression in our actions.

A high level of energy and passion. When a person's heart is captured by a need, and the team's mission is something he or she cares deeply about, there is an energy that flows from within because he or she was made for this.

An integration of roles and spiritual gifts. The particular roles people play on the team are consistent with the gifts God has given them to make the contribution they were designed to make.

Care for partners in ministry. Team members intentionally build relationships of mu-

tual concern while attempting something big for God.

Mutual ownership of ministry. Team members who have a chance to shape the mission, make time commitments and exercise gifts become equal owners of the ministry.

Transformation by the power of Christ. Teams function close to the needs they are meeting in ministry and service. Not only are the needs of others being addressed, but team members are being stretched. God transforms people when they are over their heads.

Ministry would be delicious if the preceding qualities were normative. Under the Holy Spirit's empowerment, you have the opportunity to create a team environment where this kind of life emerges. Teams are designed to reflect the original community of the trinitarian God, into whose life we tap as the body of Christ.

---

[1]Shirley Guthrie, *Greek-English Lexicon,* quoted in George Cladis, *Leading the Team-Based Church* (San Francisco: Jossey-Bass, 1999), p. 4..
[2]Cladis, *Leading the Team-Based Church,* p. 6.
[3]Elton Trueblood, *The Incendiary Fellowship* (New York: Harper & Row, 1967), p. 41.
[4]Gilbert Bilezikian, *Community 101* (Grand Rapids: Zondervan, 1997), p. 155.
[5]Ibid., p. 155.
[6]Ibid., p. 163.
[7]Cladis, *Leading the Team-Based Church,* p. 12.
[8]Paul R. Ford, *Knocking Over the Leadership Ladder* (St. Charles, Ill.: ChurchSmart Resources, 2006).
[9]Ibid., p. 14.

Leadership Exercise:
Developing a Ministry Team Covenant

Use the following instructions to walk through the *Ministry Team Covenant Worksheet* on page 79 as a group so that you can create a covenant together.

1. Go through each element of the covenant worksheet by responding to the covenanting questions in each section. Everyone's perspective is vital, and you need to hear from everyone. If you are the group leader, it might be best for you to wait until others have had a chance to share their perspective. This is particularly true if you are a pastor or the recognized head of a parachurch ministry.

2. The group's goal is to find the common ground on which all can agree. This will usually involve several iterations. Put in writing the sense of the group's shared thoughts and/or crystallize key opinions that differ.

3. Look at the written summary as a group. Discuss whether this is consistent with what you agreed to. Reflect on whether you've adequately addressed varying perspectives on key issues in the summary statement.

4. Incorporate any refinements. Build on what you have in common as you attempt to resolve the differences. Prayerfully consider what you can compromise on and what is central to your convictions.

5. It is particularly important that there is a shared understanding of the mission of the group, for that is the basis for the group participation.

6. As a *leadership exercise,* report the answers to the following questions:

What was this experience like for you? For the group? What was hard? What was life-giving?

What benefits have you seen or are you seeing?

How has this covenanting process assisted in engaging all the team members in their contribution?

Going Deeper

Cladis, George. *Leading the Team-Based Church*. San Francisco: Jossey-Bass, 1999.
Hestenes, Roberta. *Turning Committees Into Communities*. Colorado Springs: NavPress, 1991.
Ott, Stan. *Transform Your Church Through Ministry Teams*. Grand Rapids: Eerdmans, 2005.

A Ministry Team Covenant Worksheet

A covenant establishes with clarity the expectations and commitments of all the members of the team so that the leader can help the team fulfill its mission. Work through each of the elements listed, using the covenant questions under each of the headings. Then put the consensus conclusions in written form so that the group members can affirm their understanding of and commitment to the covenant. Please date each version of the covenant.

1. The mission or purpose of this team is . . . (This is usually stated in the form of "to _____" [an active verb such as *go, nurture, care for, empower,* etc.].)

   * To whom are we seeking to minister?

   * What are the needs of the people we are called to minister?

   * How would you define the mission of this team?

2. The goals for 20__ (year) are _____

   * What are your specific expectations or hopes?

   * What must you experience in order to make it worth your while?

3. Team meetings

   * When, where and for how long will the team meet?

   * What will it take to carry out the mission of this team?

4. The structure of team meetings (elements and format)

   * We will study _____ to accomplish our mission.

   * We will care for each other by _____.

   * Our regular schedule will include _____.

   * We will cultivate prayer by _____.

5. The team will review and renew this covenant on _____ [date].
   - How long should our initial covenant be? (3 months? 6 months?)

   - How often should we review and renew our covenant?

6. Team member's responsibilities:
   - Leader: what is your understanding of the role of the leader on this team?

   Who will be encouraged to be a leader in training?

   - The role of each member is _____.

   What contribution can you see yourself bringing to this team?

   What roles are needed for this team to function best? How might a particular role match your spiritual gifts?

   - Assignments between team meetings:

   How can I carry out my role and make a contribution to the team mission between team gatherings?

   - Commitments—I understand that my commitment to the team includes
     - regular attendance at all agreed meetings
     - confidentiality (what is shared in the group stays in the group)
     - active participation (I have a defined role)

   Date _____

6 / Stewarding

LOOKING AHEAD

Memory Verse: Mark 3:13-15
Bible Study: Romans 12:1-8
Reading: When Christ Calls
Leadership Exercise: Stewarding Your Personal Call

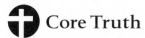 Core Truth

What is the call Christ issues to his leaders?

Christ calls leading disciples to root themselves in a daily relationship with him, to go forth on a life-transforming mission and to invest their lives in a particular and personal way consistent with the gifts God has given them. As leaders become aware of and answer Christ's call, they discover the joyful meaning and influence for which God has made them.

1. Identify key words or phrases in the question and answer above, and state their meaning in your own words.

> "THE WORLD HAS YET TO SEE WHAT GOD CAN DO WITH A [PERSON] FULLY CONSECRATED TO HIM."
>
> Words spoken by Edward Kimball to D. L. Moody, igniting Moody's sense of calling, from *A Passion for Souls* by Lyle W. Dorsett

2. Restate the core truth in your own words.

3. What questions or issues does the core truth raise for you?

Memory Verse Study Guide

Copy the entire text here:

Memory Verse: Mark 3:13-15

The leadership of Jesus was revealed in the quality of his servant love and his commitment to building a team of people who would extend that love into the world. In our memory verse we get a picture of the particular "call" Christ gave to his followers.

1. *Putting it in context.* These verses follow right on the heels of a passage that describes the huge crowds of needy people that came to Jesus for help. What do you think Jesus may have felt as he looked at this massive need?

2. What do you make of the significance of the phrase in verse 13 that says Jesus "called to him those he wanted"?

   What do you think of the idea that Jesus wants you?

3. The text says that Jesus "called" and they "came." What does this tell us about Jesus and his leading disciples?

4. Verses 14-15 suggest that the call Jesus issues has a "come" and a "go" dimension to it. What does it mean to you to come "be with Jesus?"

   What are the leading disciples sent out to do?

5. In what sense might you imagine yourself going out to do these two things?

Inductive Bible Study Guide

Bible Study: Romans 12:1-8

Romans 12 presents one of the most luminous pictures of the character of a Christian leader's life and the amazing quality of community God seeks to form through such leaders. In the first eight verses Paul speaks of God's remarkable *call* to his disciples to use their spiritual gifts to serve the body of Christ.

1. What is the "view" (v. 1) Paul regards as the starting place for a leader's life, and why is that view important?

   How has God been merciful to you, and how does this reality affect the way you live?

2. The call to be a "living sacrifice" is the *first* outcome of seeing what God has done and is doing (v. 1). As a leader, what does it mean to you to be a "living sacrifice"? (What does that look like in practice?)

   > "THE KEY TO LEADERSHIP . . . IS NOT HOW A LEADER MANAGES OTHERS, BUT HOW A LEADER MANAGES HIM- OR HERSELF."
   >
   > Edwin Friedman,
   > *A Failure of Nerve*

3. Verse 2 identifies the *second* outcome of seeing what God has done and is doing (v. 2). In what ways are you no longer conforming to the pattern of this world but being transformed?

4. According to Paul's statements in verses 1-2, what are the benefits of responding to the action and call of God upon your life?

   How has this benefited you?

5. Having described this high vision of the Christian's calling, Paul offers a sober warning in verse 3. Why do you think a leader (like you) needs to maintain both the high vision and the sober judgment Paul describes?

6. How would you describe the "big idea" that Paul is trying to convey in verses 4-8?

Describe the "gifts" God has given to you.

Where are you actually using these gifts?

7. What other questions or issues does this passage raise for you?

👓 Reading: When Christ Calls

The story is told of a roadwork crew that received the call to relieve another crew that had been digging a trench along a rural road. The foreman who had been there all day gave the new workers the task of carving out a ditch four feet deep and thirty feet long. An hour later, a neat trench had been dug. The foreman then instructed the workers to fill in the ditch. Next he had them move several yards down the road and instructed them to begin digging another trench of similar proportions.

Two hours later this time, the ditch was completed, and again the crew was asked to fill it in, move further down the road and repeat the exercise. By this time, the workers were tired and angry, and the quality of their work had deteriorated badly. When the foreman again gave the order to fill the ditch and move on, a veritable mutiny ensued.

It dawned on the foreman that he had forgotten to tell the crew *why* they had been called to this task. "Do you see that building over there?" asked the foreman, pointing across the road to an old rambling house a quarter-mile away. "That's an orphanage. Sixty children live there. Apparently, there's a crack in the water line that runs under this road and supplies those kids. Runoff from this cow pasture has gotten into the line and is making children sick. Our job is to find that break and help those kids get well."

Thirty minutes later, a neat trench four feet deep and *fifty* feet long was finished. The water line was found. The break was repaired. Not a soul on that crew thought a drop of their sweat had been wasted at all.

THE POWER OF A CALL

What a difference it makes when we are not simply doing a job but are pursuing a call to something significant! Hearing such a call is like finding treasure in the midst of life's trenches. It can transform a ditch into a place of destiny. In his book *The Call,* Os Guinness observes:

> Deep in our hearts, we all want to find and fulfill a purpose bigger than ourselves. Only such a larger purpose can inspire us to heights we know we could never reach on our own. For each of us the real purpose is personal and passionate: to know what we are here to do, and why. Kierkegaard [the Danish philosopher] wrote in his journal: "The thing is to understand myself, to see what God really wants me to do; the thing is to find a truth which is true for me, to find the idea for which I can live and die."[1]

Christian leaders are people who have discovered (or are discovering) their calling and are stewarding it carefully. Like the servants in Jesus' parable of the talents (Matthew 25:14-30), they know that the Master has given them certain treasures and called them to invest those gifts in a particular way. Their desire to please God makes them eager to remain on the job, even when they face hardships or opposition.

RECOVERING THE BIBLICAL CONCEPT OF CALL

Sadly, "calling" (or Christian vocation) is often associated with a very narrow class of leaders. Clergy are thought of as "having a call." The foreign missionary or the parachurch worker is someone who is "called." Yet when the apostle Peter says, "you are a chosen people, a royal priesthood" (1 Peter 2:9), he is addressing *all* the people of the church—financiers and homemakers, salespeople and professionals, service workers, executives and more. A tradesman himself by training, Peter urges us to remember that each one of us is called by God, and this call imbues our life with a more-than-ditch-deep purpose.

So what is this purpose? What is God's call to you, and how do you discover it? In discussing these matters, the Bible depicts three crucial dimensions of God's "call." While the concept of "call" is often associated with "hearing," there is also a sense in which discovering one's vocation as a leader is a matter of learning to "see" more clearly (Matthew 13:16; Mark 8:18). Think of the following three dimensions of *call* as lenses through which God's light shines in and through your life. There is

- the communion call—to *come* to the Foreman

- the mission call—to *go* join the Foreman's crew

- the personal call—to *invest* the gifts God has given, to do the spadework required to meet a particular need

When all three of these lenses are lined up, one over the other, God's light is intensified to an almost laserlike focus and power. Let's think about each of those lenses in turn.

The communion call (come). Mark's Gospel tells us of a particularly strategic moment in the earthly ministry of Jesus. The time came for Jesus to select the twelve persons who would become his leading disciples. This is how Mark describes the moment: "Jesus went up on a mountainside and called to him those he wanted, and they came to him. He ap-

> "VOCATION IS WHERE THE WORLD'S DEEP HUNGER AND YOUR DEEP GLADNESS MEET."
>
> Frederick Buechner, *Wishful Thinking*

pointed twelve—designating them apostles—that they might be with him" (Mark 3:13-14).

Significantly, the first call of Jesus to the world's most influential leaders-in-the-making was not "go" or "do" but "come." Jesus didn't say, "Get out there on the field and play!" or "Make an action plan and get with it!" Jesus' first call to those future, history-altering leaders was "Come unto me. Come learn of me. Come be with me." In other words, "Come, commune with me."

Jesus calls us to what Dallas Willard and Henry Blackaby describe as an interactive love relationship with him. He invites us to an ongoing journey through which we learn of him (Matthew 11:28-30). This apprenticeship is experienced within and built most profoundly upon the fellowship of other "disciples" (learners)—in communion with what Jesus called his body (the church). Through this ongoing communion with Christ and his body, a leader enters into a process of personal transformation into Christlikeness.

Jesus said, "If you remain in me and I in you, you will bear much fruit; [for] apart from me you can do nothing" (John 15:5 TNIV). You can certainly be a business leader or a political leader, a civic leader or even a church leader without answering this call. But if you want to be the kind of leader that Jesus shapes and uses most profoundly, then the first step is answering the communion call.

The mission call (go). Our highest purpose or calling is to live in communion with Christ. But it is impossible to live in the company of

Christ and not be moved outward toward the people Christ loves (see chap. 8). In other words, *coming* to Jesus inevitably moves us to *go* in his name. Being filled with Christ's character results in our being moved by Christ's concern for the world. Mark's Gospel tells us that "He appointed twelve—designating them apostles—that they might be with him . . . and that he might send them out" (Mark 3:14-15).

The word *apostle* literally means "sent one." Jesus sent his disciples to join his mission in the world. The word *mission* emphasizes this outward movement. It comes from the Greek word *missio* which means "to send." What is helpful to notice, however, are the two critical purposes for which Jesus sends out his disciples.

- Jesus sends leaders "to preach" (Mark 3:14). Seeing this, you may think: *What does preaching have to do with my life as a leader?* The word *preach* conjures the image of someone haranguing people who don't want to listen. It suggests the role played by a few specialized people. But that's not what the word originally meant, and it certainly was not what Jesus had in mind. To "preach" was simply to proclaim the good news of God's redemption and renewal through Christ. And this kind of communication can take many forms.

God gave the mission of proclamation to more than one profession or one type of personality. It wasn't given to expressive Simon Peter alone, but also to contemplative Andrew, poetic John and analytical Thomas. The list of apostles we find in Mark 3:16-19 is a study in diversity. The genius of God's plan is that he has equipped his body with a staggering variety of voices, each particularly suited to reach particular people in particular places that one person alone may never reach.

- Jesus also sends leaders with "authority to drive out demons" (Mark 3:15). Again, you may think, *What could this possibly have to do with me? Are you saying that I'm supposed to become an exorcist?* Well, that *may* be your "personal call," but not necessarily. In a larger sense Christ is simply calling his disciples to confront evil. Jesus raises up leaders who will devote themselves to casting evil out of the places it has taken up residence.

Some years ago God called Carl, a Christian, into the upper management of one of the largest media companies in the world. Though it is a company that does a great deal of good, it also markets a large number of violent films and music that feeds brutality and bitterness. Carl waited patiently and prayed for an opportunity to exercise some Christian influence over this problem. At long last an opening arose for him to question, graciously but firmly, the company's policies regarding such media content.

When he raised this challenge, opponents immediately trumpeted the artists' First Amendment right to free expression. Many would have backed off in the face of such "authoritative" claims. But Carl knew he came in the name of a higher "authority." He countered with a memorandum to the chairman of the corporation, contending that just because a musician had the right to produce vile content, the company was not bound to distribute it. Mysteriously, over the months that followed, the percentage of violent content accepted by the media division dropped significantly. Instead of making a hit, evil was taking a hit for a change.

In how many other companies, communities and even churches is the bad news (evil) being sung loudly? Where are the Christian leaders who proclaim good news and who act with humble authority to push the darkness back?

The personal call (invest). Strengthened by communion with Christ and his body, inspired by the mission Jesus gave, Christian leaders must also answer a very personal call. "What is the *particular job* that you have given me to do, O Master Foreman? Why did you put me here by *this roadside?*" Often, the key to answering these questions lies in examining the "shovel" you've been gifted with. God has a personal call for you—a specific need that you are meant to address—and the key to discovering it lies in studying the gifts God has already placed in your heart and hands. Think about this in terms of the acrostic word G-I-F-T.

- Consider your *grace* gifts. Do you remember the first time you went from using an ordinary screwdriver or saw to using a power tool? In high school shop class, I (Dan) remember endlessly rubbing a woodcraft project with sandpaper, only to see some other kids doing their work with a belt-sander. *Where do I get one of those?* I wondered! The Bible teaches that when someone becomes a follower of Jesus Christ, God endows that person with certain "spiritual gifts" that function like power tools for completing the work God has given them to do. In Romans 12:6 Paul says: "We have different gifts, according to the grace given us." In Ephesians 4:7 Paul underlines this again by saying, "to each one of us grace has been given as Christ apportioned it." In other words, in God's shop everyone gets power tools!

Do you know what yours are? In Romans 12

Paul lists among those "grace gifts" the ability to speak a word of truth from the Lord to people, the capacity to encourage people, the gift of teaching or leading or administrating. He lists the ability to serve quietly or to express mercy or to make money and contribute it generously as forms of spiritual gifts. Understanding how you've been grace-gifted can help you begin to discern your personal call.

- Consider your *insights* and inspirations (passions). The gifts God has given you to discern and fulfill your call also include the *passions* you've developed over the course of your education, your work and life experience, and God's other dealings with you along the way. You may have a burning insight or feel a nagging inspiration about a particular concern. *Why doesn't anybody do something about that problem?* you wonder. *It seems so obvious to me that something could be done in this area,* you think. *Somebody really ought to . . .* you muse.

When we finally say yes to this call, it may be costly. Like Jesus, "who for the joy set before him endured the cross" (Hebrews 12:2), however, a Christian leader feels a fire in the belly that can't be put out even when adversity rains down. Like Jesus, who told the disciples when they were concerned that he had skipped a meal, "My food is to do the will of him who sent me and to finish his work" (John 4:34), a leader will often feel nourished by fixing a problem or seizing a ministry opportunity.

William Wilberforce was a member of the British Parliament in the late 1700s. After his conversion to Christ, he continued his aristocratic, self-centered lifestyle until he realized he was still living without a higher purpose. He wrote in his journal, "The first years I was in Parliament, I did nothing—nothing that is to any purpose. My own distinction was my darling object." So he asked God for a purpose to make a difference. On October 28, 1787, he made this notation in his journal, "God has set before me two great objects, the suppression of the slave trade and the reformation of manners [or morals]." God led Wilberforce to the need he was created to address, and in answering this personal call he was instrumental in ending slavery in the British Empire.

Not all of us, of course, will have such far-reaching calls—but there is *some* need or opportunity in your church, your community, your circle of influence or even in the world beyond about which you will have a burning insight and are inspired to act, a sense of passion that "for *this* I was made."

- Consider your *form*. You are a unique being, and even if you have an identical twin, there will never be another person exactly like you. God has shaped your personality and temperament in a particular way and this form is intentional. Just look at the stunning variety of characters Jesus first selected for his service: from doubting Thomas to aggressive Peter to sensitive John to compulsive Martha and outgoing Mary. We almost get the im-pression that Christ was purposely assembling a mosaic of personalities, each offering something that could advance his purposes in the church and world.

Rick Warren suggests that the people of God are like different pieces of stained glass through which the light of the Lord pours in brilliant array. Sometimes pastors stand in their churches and feel like they're standing in the middle of Notre Dame Cathedral watching God's light pour through the rose window. The "glass" that is you may need polishing. It may be cracked or chipped in places. But your form matters. The more you understand your personality, temperament and strengths, the easier it will be to discern your personal call.

- Consider your *treasure*. Jesus told us that we could learn a lot about our heart by reflecting on our treasure. "For where your treasure is, there your heart will be also" (Matthew 6:21). The way we amass and invest our money and possessions can suggest something about where our passion and gifting lies. These things tell us what we truly care about and what we're good at. It's important to remember also that our money and possessions may be one of the "shovels" or "talents" God has given us in order to address a particular need. Hud, a businessman in a church in northern California came to discern his call partly in this way. His story is worth sharing.

ONE LEADER'S JOURNEY

In 1989, after the fall of the Romanian dictator Nicolae Ceausescu, it was discovered that thousands of orphans had been warehoused in absolutely atrocious conditions. One of the many orphanages, a place simply called PC3, was located in the port city of Constanta on the Black Sea. Thirty-five HIV-positive kids lived there, all of them under six years old. They experienced the deprivation of abandonment, a criminally backward hospital system and neglect from uncaring aids.

In 1992 Hud said yes to going on a short-term mission trip that took him to that orphanage in Constanta. He openly expressed fear of being exposed to these children. A successful commercial real estate developer, Hud, age forty-five, was financially secure—

free to spend his days pursuing his hobbies of hang-gliding and golf. But what if the needs of these children penetrated his heart and disturbed his comfortable life? On this trip, Hud's fears were realized. During a prayer time in Romania, Hud suddenly broke down, sobbing uncontrollably over the plight of these children.

From 1992 to 1996, Hud found himself drawn back to PC3 many times. Each time he visited, he became more aware of and frustrated by the predicament of the kids. As he entered the orphanage one day, he found that the children had been shoved into a room where a video of the film *Platoon* was playing. Seven- and eight-year-old children were watching scenes of unspeakable violence and chaos. There were no adult attendants anywhere. As he looked into the eyes of the children, Hud could see them asking, "Are you the one? Are you the one who will finally help us or will you abandon us like everyone else?"

The question burned in Hud's heart. He realized that deep, systemic problems had to be addressed. Something big and dramatic had to be done for these conditions to change. The orphanage would need to be wrestled away from the state and placed under the leadership of capable, Christian people. Suddenly, Hud's sense of call came into focus— like perfectly aligned lenses with the laser light shining through. Hud instinctively knew, *I must do this.*

Over the next two years Hud used the negotiating skills he'd developed in the commercial real estate business to wrest control of the orphanage from the Romanian government. In 1998, PC3 became *Casa Viata Noua* (House of New Life). Today, Romanian Christians direct the ministry. The children live in family units of three to five, and each family is cared for by two mothers who maintain a long-term relationship with the children.

This was accomplished by one man who responded to God's call on his life. He had no training in child development and no background in medicine. But he was in *communion* with Christ; he had a sense of his *mission* and was open to allowing the gifts God had given him at a *personal* level to meet the need of the world.

AMAZING GRACE

Paul says in 1 Corinthians 12: "God works in different ways, but it is the same God who does the work in all of us" (v. 6 NLT). That's good news, isn't it—that there is Someone besides us that does the heaviest lifting? Usually, God's call is something that can't be fulfilled without God acting supernaturally in some way. The Bible tells us that Abraham was conscious of this (Genesis 12:1-6). Moses and Mary were too (Exodus 3—4; Luke 1:26-38. Carl and Hud and so many others could tell you their own stories. If you feel inadequate to address a need fully through your own resources, chances are that you are in a fine position to be used of God.

The great news for all would-be leaders is that when a disciple is willing to answer the *communion* call and the *mission* call, and invest their gifts in the direction of the *personal* call, God supplies the grace. As the apostle Paul learned in his own experience as a leader, God "is able to do immeasurably more than all we ask or imagine, according to his power that is at work within us" (Ephesians 3:20).

---

[1]Os Guinness, *The Call* (Nashville: Word Publishing, 1998), p. 3.

Leadership Exercise: Stewarding Your Personal Call

God has given you a G-I-F-T—a specific shovel and a ditch to dig—that will make a profound difference in the ministry of your church or in Christ's mission in the world. People are going to be blessed by God through you. Pray, asking God to awaken you to the way he has made you and to the call he has given you. Then answer the following questions as God gives you light to do so.

1. My grace gifts.* I think I may have been supernaturally gifted with a capacity for:

___ *Craftsmanship*. I am able to use my hands and mind to build up the kingdom through artistic, creative means (Exodus 28:3-4).

___ *Hospitality*. I feel deeply alive when I am opening my home to offer lodging, food and fellowship to other people (Genesis 18:1-15).

___ *Faith/Exhortation*. I am able to provide other people with unusual confidence in God's presence, promises and power—to such an extent that they come to rely more on this (Acts 11:23-24; 14:21-22; Hebrews 11).

___ *Discernment*. I feel unusually able to know whether some behavior or direction is of God or of someone or something else (Acts 5:3-6; Acts 16:16-18).

___ *Mercy*. I feel exceptional empathy and compassion for those who are suffering and a willingness to devote considerable time and energy to alleviate it (Luke 10:30-37).

___ *Giving*. I delight in offering my material blessings for God's work in the church or world (2 Corinthians 8:1-5).

___ *Administration*. I am able to describe and deliver the processes and structures needed to help a team of people achieve goals that advance God's work in the church or the world (Acts 15:12-21).

___ *Leadership*. I am able to motivate, direct and support people in such a way that they effectively work together to advance God's purposes (Exodus 18:13-16; Judges 3:10; Hebrews 13:7).

___ *Helps/Service*. I enjoy meeting practical needs or helping others do their tasks more effectively and don't really care whether I am in the limelight or not (Acts 6:2-4; Galatians 6:1-2).

___ *Knowledge/Wisdom*. I am able to understand in an exceptional way the great truths of God's Word and to make them relevant to specific situations (Ephesians 3:14-19 ; James 3:13-17).

___ *Music*. I delight in praising God through choral or instrumental music and can enhance the worship experience of others (Mark 14:26; 1 Corinthians 14:26).

___ *Teaching*. I am able to communicate the truths of God's Word so that others learn from it (Hebrews 5:12-14).

___ *Pastoring/Shepherding*. I enjoy assuming responsibility for the spiritual welfare of a group of people and long to see them grow in faith and discipleship (1 Peter 5:1-11).

---

*Our thanks to CforC Ministries for the basic framework for this list of grace gifts.

___ *Evangelism.* I find pleasure in sharing the gospel with nonbelievers in such a way that they become disciples of Jesus (Acts 8:26-40).

___ *Prophecy.* I am able to interpret and apply God's revelation in a given situation (1 Corinthians 14:1-5, 30-33, 37-40).

___ *Apostleship.* I have a passionate heart for planting or developing churches and Christian ministries by the proclamation and the teaching of biblical doctrine and practical discipleship. (Acts 13:1-5; 14:21-23).

___ *Crosscultural Mission.* I get unusually excited by the opportunity to use my spiritual gifts in a culture other than my primary one (1 Corinthians 9:19-23).

___ *Healing.* I find that God uses me to restore spiritual or physical health to the sick (Luke 9:1-2; James 5:13-16).

___ *Intercession.* I like to pray for extended periods of time with great positive effect for the building of God's kingdom. (1 Thessalonians 3:10-13; 1 Timothy 2:1-2).

2. My insights and inspirations. My mind and heart race when I contemplate _____.
I feel a sense of positive burden or oughtness about _____.
I am moved by people who are seriously addressing _____.
I am deeply disturbed and excited by the following needs in the church:

in the world:

3. My form.

I know the following things about my personality and temperament that have a bearing on where and how I lead and serve:

When it comes to leadership, some of my best assets (strengths) are:

When it comes to leadership, some of my greatest liabilities (sins) are:

4. My treasure. I have the following material resources that I could invest in the purposes of God:

PUTTING IT ALL TOGETHER

1. Are you confused about where you might focus your leadership G-I-F-Ts or does a picture form? How would you describe what you are thinking?

2. Who do you need to speak or partner with to take the next step in acting further on God's personal call to you?

3. What questions do you have about the reading?

4. Does the reading convict, challenge, or comfort you? Why?

Going Deeper

Self-awareness is a key to leadership. Strong leaders know where their strengths and limitations lie. In discerning your *form,* the following resources may help:

The StrengthsFinder Inventory
Buckingham, Marcus, and Donald Clifton. *Now Discover Your Strengths*. New York: Free Press, 2001. See also <www.strengthsfinder.com>.

The DISC Inventory
<www.resourcesunlimited.com/DiSC_Profiles.asp>
<www.discprofile.com>

The Myers-Briggs Profile
<www.myersbriggs.org>

The Enneagram Profile
Riso, Don Richard, and Russ Hudson. *Discovering Your Personality Type*. New York: Houghton-Mifflin, 2003. See also <www.enneagraminstitute.com>.

Exercising leadership with one's *treasure* is also a broadly explored theme of Scripture. The following materials on stewardship provide particularly practical and readable insights into these topics:

Alcorn, Randy. *The Treasure Principle*. Sisters Ore.: Multnomah, 2001.

Dayton, Howard. *Your Money Counts*. Carol Stream, Ill.: Tyndale House, 1996.

Sutherland, Dave, and Kirk Nowery. *The 33 Laws of Stewardship*. Camarillo: New Source Publishing, 2003.

Part Three

The Vision of a Leader

A visionary is someone who helps people see what they probably would not be able to see on their own. A great artist paints scenes that the viewer can vicariously enter into. Leaders do the same. Leaders share a journey with people that takes them into a preferred future. Most people must be aroused from their lethargy in order to rise to a previously unattainable or unthinkable level. Therefore a leader's vision must come with a sense of urgency if people are to be moved from complacency to engage in a mission that requires total commitment.

In order for a leader to help others to see, they must first have a vision. Leaders can talk only about what they already see. Christian leadership is often viewed in terms of some lofty Moses-like vision of a promised land. But Christian leadership also includes picturing the present reality in the kingdom of God. Thus this unit begins with two foundational realities before discussing the vision of a preferred future.

The compelling Christ (chap. 7). Vision begins not with Christ's vision for us but our vision of him. The most important reality that a leader can point to is the captivating and magnetic nature of Jesus Christ. The nineteenth-century French novelist Victor Hugo said of his bishop, "He did not study God, he was dazzled by Him." What do Christian leaders most desire? That the people they serve are dazzled by Jesus Christ. We follow him into eternity. As we get closer to Jesus, we are both reassured and disturbed. Whenever we think we have him figured out, he throws us off-balance; he never ceases to amaze us.

The kingdom of God (chap. 8). Jesus preached the enigmatic "kingdom of God." With him came a new regime that was present yet still future. Though his kingdom would reside in his followers, it came from the future into this present darkness. This unseen rule of God came to displace the kingdom of darkness and to announce that the future has triumphed. This mysterious kingdom, though a hidden reality, is surer than the empirical world. We live in the atmosphere of this kingdom; it is the air we breathe and gives us hope. Thus we pray as Jesus taught us, "your kingdom come, your will be done on earth as it is in heaven" (Matthew 6:10).

Helping others see (chap. 9). If we lack a vision of the compelling Christ or the sense that God's kingdom extends to the ends of the earth, we don't have the proper foundation for helping others see. Much of what we want to help others see is that Jesus Christ is a confounding, charismatic figure in whom there is life, and that he came preaching the reign of God, which is at odds with this present world. Once we see these truths, we can ask God for the role that our particular ministry can play in the grand scheme of God's plan. Vision is the ability to see and help others to see and embrace the mission God has called us to accomplish.

7 / The Compelling Christ

LOOKING AHEAD

Memory Verse: Colossians 1:15-20
Bible Study: Revelation 1:9-18
Reading: The Confounding Christ
Leadership Exercise: Keeping the Confounding Christ Alive Before and in Us

 Core Truth

What is the fundamental priority of leading disciples?

Above all else leading disciples seek to be captivated by the presence and power of the person of Jesus Christ. As lifelong apprentices Christian leaders place themselves under Christ's formative influence so that they live as if Christ were living his life through them.

1. Identify key words or phrases in the question and answer above, and state their meaning in your own words.

2. Restate the core truth in your own words.

3. What questions or issues does the core truth raise for you?

Memory Verse Study Guide

Copy the entire text here:

Memory Verse: Colossians 1:15-20

Though the truth of the incarnation is at the heart of the wonder of Christ, the cosmic claims about Christ rivet our fascination and reverence. The apostle Paul tells us in Colossians 1:15-20 that Jesus is the final word about God, creation and redemption.

1. What terms or phrases does the apostle Paul use to affirm Christ's deity?

2. How is Paul using the phrase "the firstborn over all creation" (v. 15)? If we interpreted this as a statement of chronology, it sounds as if Jesus was the "first to be born" in creation. How else could the term *firstborn* be used here? (Feel free to consult a commentary or study Bible.)

3. According to Paul, what is Jesus' relationship to creation?

4. Read Colossians 1:17. Dwell on the phenomenal phrase "in him all things hold together." What do you suppose Paul has in mind here?

5. At the heart of Jesus' work of redemption is reconciliation (v. 20). The need for reconciliation indicates that both parties are at odds with each other. What is the nature of the animosity between humanity and God, and how did Jesus provide reconciliation?

6. Summarize in your own words the breadth of the claims that Paul makes about Jesus Christ.

Inductive Bible Study Guide

Bible Study: Revelation 1:9-18

The apostle John allows us to peek at the revelation of Jesus Christ that he was given while in exile on the island of Patmos, off the Southwest coast of modern-day Turkey. Scholars date the book of Revelation to the A.D. 90s. At this time the Roman emperor Domitian ordered his subjects to worship him as Lord and God, *Dominus et Deus*. He changed the name of the Roman Empire to the "Eternal Empire" and called himself "Everlasting King." All Roman subjects were required to go to a temple built in Domitian's honor, throw incense on altar and declare "Caesar is Lord." It is against this backdrop that John receives a dramatic visitation of the true Lord and God.

1. Revelation 1:9 gives us the reasons for John's being in exile. Restate these reasons in your own words.

2. According to verses 10-11, what is the context and purpose for the revelation of Jesus Christ?

3. When John turns to see who was speaking, he saw one "like the son of man" among the seven lampstands (representing the seven churches—see Revelation 1:20). In your commentary or study Bible, look up the eight word pictures used to describe Jesus (vv. 13-16) and state what the picture conveys about him.

    • "dressed in a robe . . . golden sash around his chest" (v. 13)

    • "head and hair were white like wool" (v. 14)

    • "his eyes were like blazing fire" (v. 14)

    • "his feet were like bronze glowing in a furnace" (v. 15)

- "his voice was like the sound of rushing waters" (v. 15)

- "in his right hand he held seven stars" (v. 16)

- "out of his mouth came a sharp double-edged sword" (v. 16)

- "his face was like the sun shining in all its brilliance" (v. 16)

4. Why do you suppose John's response to this revelation was to fall "at his feet as though dead" (v. 17)?

5. What do Jesus' comforting words tell us about him? (vv. 17-18)

6. How does this picture of Jesus inform the image of him that you will keep as a follower and leader?

"JESUS' ENDURING RELEVANCE IS BASED ON HIS HISTORICALLY PROVEN ABILITY TO SPEAK TO, TO HEAL AND EMPOWER THE INDIVIDUAL HUMAN CONDITION. HE MATTERS BECAUSE OF WHAT HE BROUGHT AND WHAT HE STILL BRINGS TO ORDINARY HUMAN BEINGS, LIVING THEIR ORDINARY LIVES AND COPING DAILY WITH THEIR SURROUNDINGS. HE PROMISES WHOLENESS FOR THEIR LIVES."

Dallas Willard, *The Divine Conspiracy*

👓 Reading: The Confounding Christ

Can't live with him; can't live without him. So it is with Jesus. As much as he affirms us, he disturbs us. As much as he gives us a singular focus, he complicates our decisions. His yoke is easy, but his way is hard. He is the confounding Christ.

Every leader must first be a disciple. Disciples leave no doubt as to who is providing the formative power in their lives. Therefore the fundamental issue for a disciple who leads is, Who is this person Jesus who is providing the "formative power" over our lives? What compels us to follow him? How do we keep this relationship alive and Jesus ever before us?

If we are to call others to follow him, we must ourselves first be captivated by the person and power of Jesus Christ. A relationship with Jesus should come with equal amounts of fear and fascination. At the same time we are drawn to the irresistible Jesus, we find ourselves pushing him away because he shows us things about ourselves that are simply too uncomfortable.

This push and pull of discipleship is illustrated dramatically in Peter and his companions' encounter with Christ (Luke 5:1-11). We will see how Jesus orchestrates the events in order to unnerve these mere mortals with his display of other-worldly authority. Jesus enters the turf of these fishermen (Peter, James and John) and upsets their comfortable, predictable existence.

Here is the backdrop against which Jesus unveils his identity. Masses of people had converged on the shore of Lake Gennesaret (also known as the Sea of Galilee) to hear Jesus' message. The sheer physical press of the crowd forces Jesus to borrow Peter's boat, which

Jesus turns into a floating pulpit.

When he's done teaching, Jesus sets up Peter with the command, "Put out into the deep water, and let down the nets for a catch" (Luke 5:4). Peter responds to this request with an exasperation born of exhaustion. He does not hide his irritation. "Master, we've worked hard all night and haven't caught anything" (Luke 5:5). In addition to Peter's sheer tiredness, you get the impression that he thinks Jesus is out of his element. Peter is a fisherman who comes from a long line of fishermen. This was his profession. Jesus shows his ignorance by his request, "Put out into deep water." Deep waters are for night fishing. Peter perhaps was thinking, *Jesus, you stick to preaching, and let us handle the fishing.*

Yet out of sheer reverence for the Master, Peter acceded to the request. "But because you say so, I will let down the nets" (Luke 5:5). Peter has sufficient respect to acquiesce, but he does not expect success. Yet no sooner had the nets been lowered into the sea than it seemed that every fish in the lake had decided its time had come. Peter signaled for his partners in another boat to help him with this catch, and yet the size of the haul threatened to sink both boats.

Our interest here is Peter's reaction to the catch of fish. If Peter had been selfishly focused solely on the financial success of this venture, he might have consulted a lawyer, drawn up a contract and tried to sign Jesus on as a full partner. Yet financial gain was the last thing Peter was thinking of.

This Jesus who confounds Peter is simultaneously disturbing and attractive. "When Simon Peter saw this, he fell at Jesus' knees and said, 'Go away from me, Lord; I am a sinful man'" (Luke 5:8). Peter is a conflicted man, experiencing what psychologists call "cognitive dissonance." Peter's words and actions collided. His life was a head-on train wreck.

On the one hand, Peter appears to be drawn to Jesus. We can picture Peter high-stepping it through the waters, running toward this man who commands the seas to obey him. Peter falls at the feet of Jesus in an act of worship. He never felt more vital than his did at that moment.

At the same time, Peter intuitively knows he is in the presence of no mere mortal. He is experiencing an excruciatingly painful exposure. "Go away from me, Lord; I am a sinful man." I don't deserve to be in your presence, Peter is saying. Leave me, for I can't seem to leave you.

I (Greg) would submit that this lifelong approach-avoidance, push-pull dynamic keeps us under the formative power of Jesus Christ. Jesus is like none other, and this is why he is so compelling.

Let's look more closely at what is going on with Peter.

Peter is repulsed by the presence of the holy One of God. What was Peter experiencing when he said, "Go away from me, Lord; I am a sinful man"? Peter had no category by which to classify Jesus Christ. He instinctively knew that this was no mere man. Somehow, in a way that his mind would never be able to explain, the Holy One of Israel was embodied in the person of Jesus. The normally hidden glory of God had for a moment been unveiled through a person, and Peter was overwhelmed.

To experience the holiness of God is to come face to face with "overpoweringness" (to coin a word). Forces had been unleashed over

which Peter had no control, and they threatened to undo him. In *Out of the Silent Planet,* C. S. Lewis describes the feeling of Ransom when Oyarsa, a god figure, moved among his subjects, "Ransom felt a tingling of his blood and pricking on his fingers as if lightning were near him; and his heart and body seemed to him to be made of water."[1]

This was Job's experience, as well. We know the story of how Job lost everything—wealth, family and health—because God allowed Satan to sift him. Job was reduced to scraping his open sores with dirty pieces of clay while his friends urged him to confess his sin, as if this was the cause of his misfortune. But Job tenaciously held to his innocence. He dared even to accuse God of injustice, claiming that he had done nothing to warrant this kind of treatment. God owed him an explanation. But nowhere does God give Job an intellectually satisfying answer for his condition. God simply breaks forth in power and pulls rank. Frederick Buechner writes: "God doesn't explain. He explodes. He asks Job who he thinks he is anyway. He says to Job that to try to explain the kinds of things Job wants explained would be like trying to explain Einstein to a little necked clam. God doesn't reveal his grand design. He reveals Himself."[2]

"Will the one who contends with the Almighty correct him?" says the Lord to Job (Job 40:2). Job is overwhelmed with God's revelation, saying:

My ears had heard of you
   but now my eyes have seen you.
Therefore I despise myself
   and repent in dust and ashes. (Job 42:5-6)

Like Job, Peter is overpowered. It is this "overpoweringness" that produced a sense of his moral corruption. "Go away from me, Lord; I am a sinful man." But why did Peter focus on his inner taintedness?

The presence of the holy pressed upon Peter. The word *holy* means "to cut or separate." In modern terminology we say someone is "a cut above." In theological language we call this "transcendence," which means to exceed the usual limits. Jesus is the one who exceeds the usual limits; he is a cut above, the standard by which everything else is measured.

Up to this point, Peter was most likely similar to other human beings, morally adrift and generally easy on himself. We tend to grade our moral quality on a curve, not against an absolute scale. Sure, we have our little foibles, bad habits, but doesn't everyone? We might think, *Certainly I am no saint, but I am generally a good sort of person.* We make the assumption that God has the same complacency about our shortcomings.

Peter no longer had that luxury. His scale of measurement had been obliterated in a matter of moments. All of his fuzzy-headed self-justification now made no difference. He stood in the presence of absolute holiness. Jesus Christ was the curve breaker. For the first time Peter saw himself from the vantage point of the holy God.

Peter stood exposed. Most of us can minimize the pain of our sin because the revealing light of God's holiness exposes our darkness a bit at a time. But Peter went immediately from blinding darkness to piercing brilliance. He

> "THE MORE I STUDIED
> JESUS, THE MORE
> DIFFICULT IT BECAME TO
> PIGEONHOLE HIM. . . . AS
> WALTER WINK HAS SAID,
> IF JESUS HAD NEVER
> LIVED, WE WOULD NOT
> HAVE BEEN ABLE TO
> INVENT HIM."
>
> Philip Yancey, *The Jesus I Never Knew*

wanted to push Jesus away; the psychic throb was too great. When we become a disciple of Jesus, we place ourselves under the gaze of God and allow him to expose our personal darkness. The good news, though, is that the very light that reveals the darkness also provides the healing.

Peter experienced Jesus as a disturbing, troubling and convicting purity who could see straight through to the depths of his soul. There was no place to hide: "Depart from me."

Peter is drawn to life-giving Jesus. On the other had, Peter's repulsion was only half the story. The other half of the story is that in Jesus we find life itself. At the same time Peter was pleading for Jesus to leave, he was on his knees worshiping him. We can envision Peter clutching onto Jesus' robe as if Peter is restraining his departure. As painful as this moment is, Peter doesn't want to be anywhere else. What a rush! He is a perfect mixture of fear and fascination. Isn't this similar to the powerful personalities we have encountered in life? They can be painfully irritating, but they are so colorful that simply being around them makes you feel more alive.

Jesus had charisma. On the day when Peter's business had never been more successful, Jesus calls him away to follow him: "For he and all his companions were astonished at the catch of fish they had taken, and so were James and John, the sons of Zebedee, Simon's partners. Then Jesus said to Simon, 'Don't be afraid; from now on you will catch men.' So they pulled their boats up on shore, left everything and followed him" (Luke 5:9-11).

There was such a captivating aura about the person of Jesus that simply being associated with him was worth the loss of financial security. Peter now felt more alive around Jesus than anyone he ever had encountered.

After one of the hard teachings of Jesus, many who had followed him began to fall away. The disciples themselves were saying, "This is a hard teaching, who can accept it?" (John 6:60). Seeing many fall away, Jesus turned to his disciples, "You do not want to leave too, do you?" (John 6:67). It was Peter who spoke for the Twelve, "Lord, to whom shall we go? You have the words of eternal life. We believe and know that you are the Holy One of God" (John 6:68-69).

Jesus' power was such that he could ask his followers to totally commit their lives to him. Planted in our heart is the desire to find something worthy of devoting our entire life to. Jesus' immeasurable worth requires the full development of our minds, the complete harnessing of our emotions and the total discipline of our wills. Jesus himself promised that "whoever loses his life for me will save it" (Luke 9:24).

Jesus called Peter and his fellow fishermen to a different kind of fishing business: "from now on you will catch men" (Luke 5:10). Jesus was giving them the opportunity to catch people for him. And then they would see him redirect these lives toward his Father, the God who was revealing himself in Jesus.

None other than God in human form was enlisting them in service of the greatest enterprise on earth. In *Knowing God,* J. I. Packer wonderfully captures the dignifying nature of this call. He tells us to imagine that we are

given the opportunity of a lifetime to meet the one person we would consider at the pinnacle—a cut above all others in rank, intellectual power, professional skill or personal sanctity. Pause and think of who that person might be for you. Visualize yourself having a private audience with this person whom you would consider a lifetime honor to meet. The more you are consciously aware of your inferiority, the more you realize it is not your place to initiate or control the conversation but to allow it to be directed by this exalted person. If this figure kept the conversation on the level of courteous pleasantries, you might be disappointed, but you certainly couldn't complain. You would still have bragging rights. But what if this person began to confide in you his or her deepest thoughts and concerns? In fact, what if he or she went beyond that and invited you to share in some personally planned undertaking, and asked if you might be available whenever the person needed you. All of a sudden you find your head lifting and your chest swelling, and you would feel alive like never before. You are a personal assistant to this great figure.

No wonder the disciples were drawn to Jesus. They were called to carry out the work of the King of the universe, who had traveled from eternity to time to establish his kingdom on earth. They were being asked to be part of his plan. His life became theirs.

PETER AND US

Peter's experience of Jesus in Luke 5 models for us what it means to be a Christian leader. First, we are to submit ourselves to the shaping influence of Jesus; we are apprentices who constantly balance the fear and fascination of living in his presence. *Discipleship Essentials* provides the following definition of a disciple: "A disciple is one who responds in faith and obedience to the gracious call of Jesus Christ. Being a disciple is a lifelong process of dying to self while allowing Jesus Christ to come alive in us."[3]

There are two daily moment-by-moment movements in a disciple's life. First there is a healthy fear before a holy God.

> Search me, O God, and know my
>   heart;
>   test me and know my anxious
>   thoughts.
> See if there is any offensive way in me.
> (Psalm 139:23-24)

With the journey inward we are inviting Jesus to take the search light of the Holy Spirit to root around in our souls and ferret out the darkness. The fascinating thing is that the closer we are drawn to the light of God's love and the more we passionately pursue a relationship with the living Christ, the more we become aware of how far we have to go. This has been the testimony of the saints down through the ages.

Second, and simultaneously, we are called to the life and work that Jesus has for us. Dallas Willard writes, "A disciple of Jesus is a person who is learning from him how to live their life in the Kingdom of God as he would live their life if he were they. A disciple is one who is with him learning to be like him."[4]

Gerhard Kittel's study on the word *disciple* says that it "always implies the existence of a personal attachment which shapes the whole life of the one described as *mathetes* [Greek for disciple], which in its particularity, leaves no doubt as to who is deploying the formative power."[5]

Jesus takes up residence in us. He cleans house over a lifetime, but at the same time he makes us fit for service in his kingdom. His work of renovation is never done. As Jesus' life is working through us, he draws us into a meaningful life of service to others. Fear and fascination. It is at this juncture that we are truly alive.

C. S. Lewis understood this balance like few have. That's why he chose the image of a lion to represent the Christ figure in The Chronicles of Narnia. When Susan and Lucy ask the Beavers if Aslan is "safe," they are told: "Safe?" said Mr. Beaver; . . . "Who said anything about safe? 'Course he isn't safe. But he's good. He's the King, I tell you."[6]

There you have the allure of discipleship in a nutshell. When we follow Jesus, he will keep messing with us. But does our body tingle when we are around anyone else as it does with him? Where else would we rather be than in the presence of this One who is unlike anyone else who has ever walked this earth?

---

[1]C. S. Lewis, *Out of the Silent Planet* (New York: Macmillan, 1970), p. 119.

[2]Frederick Buechner, *Wishful Thinking* (San Francisco: Harper San Francisco, 1993), p. 46.

[3]Greg Ogden, *Discipleship Essentials* (Downers Grove, Ill.: InterVarsity Press, 1998), p. 24.

[4]Dallas Willard, unpublished notes (Oak Brook, Ill.: Oak Brook Conference on Ministry: Renovating the Heart, November, 2005).

[5]Gerhard Kittel, "Mathetes," *Theological Dictionary of the New Testament* (Grand Rapids: Eerdmans, 1997), p. 441.

[6]C. S. Lewis, *The Lion, the Witch, and the Wardrobe* (New York: Macmillan, 1957), p. 64.

Leadership Exercise: Keeping the Confounding Christ Alive Before and in Us

In the most basic sense a disciple is simply an apprentice to a master. But in the sense that believers in Christ are disciples, we are apprentices to the Master. In Jesus' day the rabbis had disciples who viewed them as the living Torah—the rule of life with skin on. We are apprentices to Jesus—God with skin on. Nothing should more captivate our life than his life and how Jesus would live his life through us. In other words, leadership is about who we are in Christ.

This leadership exercise focuses on developing a plan to always keep before us the balance of fear and fascination with the person of Jesus Christ.

1. Assess where you currently are with Jesus Christ. In all honesty, how would you describe who Jesus Christ is at this moment in your life? Check all the following that apply:

    ___ I am captivated by him.

    ___ He seems distant/remote.

    ___ He's just there.

    ___ I need greater knowledge of him.

    ___ I'm growing my appreciation for him.

    ___ I want to get closer to him.

    ___ I find him stunning.

    ___ I'm confused about him.

    ___ I'm not sure what he requires of me.

    ___ He is the love of my life.

    ___ My life is compartmentalized.

    ___ Jesus is a historical figure to me.

    ___ I find him compelling.

    ___ He is worth dying for.

    ___ Other:_____

    From what you have marked, write a description of who Jesus is to you now and the place he presently has in your life.

2. Do you agree or disagree? Jesus remains the compelling figure in our life when we keep fear and fascination in balance. Explain.

3. How do you intend to keep your life before the exposing light of Christ's presence so that he can root out the darkness?

4. Dallas Willard writes, "A disciple of Jesus is a person who is learning from him to live their life in the Kingdom of God as he would live their life if he were they. A disciple is one who is with him learning to be like him." What aspect of the person of Jesus Christ is most fascinating to you now? How does this quality get embodied into your life (e.g., the way he loved his enemies)?

5. Kittel's provocative definition of a disciple concludes that a disciple "leaves no doubt as to who is deploying the formative power." In your life, what practices would you have to develop in order to leave no doubt that Jesus is deploying the formative power?

In your life, what specific challenges in thought, feelings or actions would demonstrate that you want Jesus to be your formative power?

> "THE STORY OF JESUS IS THE STORY OF A CELEBRATION, A STORY OF LOVE. . . . JESUS EMBODIES THE PROMISE OF A GOD WHO WILL GO TO ANY LENGTH TO WIN US BACK. . . . THE NOVELIST AND LITERARY CRITIC REYNOLDS PRICE PUT IT THIS WAY: 'HE SAYS IN THE CLEAREST VOICE WE HAVE THE SENTENCE THAT MANKIND CRAVES FROM STORIES—*THE MAKER OF ALL THINGS LOVES AND WANTS ME.*'"
>
> Philip Yancey, *The Jesus I Never Knew*

Going Deeper

Lewis, C. S. *Mere Christianity*. New York: Macmillan, 1977.

Yancey. Philip. *The Jesus I Never Knew*. Grand Rapids: Zondervan, 2002.

8 / Embracing the Kingdom

LOOKING AHEAD

Memory Verse: Mark 1:14-15
Bible Study: Matthew 11:1-13
Reading: Adopters of the Kingdom of God
Leadership Exercise: Assessing Your Kingdom Vision

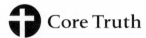 Core Truth

What is a leading disciple's worldview?

Christian leadership is founded on a faithful adoption of and a forceful adaptation to the reality and rules of the kingdom of God. This kingdom is God's presence and power breaking into human personality and culture to bring about the glorious renewal of life.

1. Identify key words or phrases in the question and answer above, and state their meaning in your own words.

2. Restate the core truth in your own words.

3. What questions or issues does the core truth raise for you?

Memory Verse Study Guide

Copy the entire text here:

Memory Verse: Mark 1:14-15

The nature and nearness of the kingdom of God is the preeminent theme in the ministry of Jesus and the foundation of Christian leadership. In our memory verse, we are given a wonderful summary of this vision.

1. *Putting it in context.* This text is the first glimpse Mark gives us of the ministry of Jesus, appearing immediately before the calling of his leading disciples. What does this say to you about the value of these verses as keys to understanding Christ's message and ministry?

2. Jesus apparently began his ministry "proclaiming the good news of God." What is "the good news of God" as you understand it?

3. Jesus ties "good news" to the coming of the "kingdom of God." What does the term *kingdom of God* mean or bring to mind for you?

4. What do you think Jesus meant when he said "The kingdom of God is near"?

5. In both the ministry of Jesus and that of his cousin John (Mark 1:4), repentance is stressed heavily. Why do you think repentance is essential to taking hold of the good news of the kingdom?

Inductive Bible Study Guide

Bible Study: Matthew 11:1-13

John the Baptist is counted by Christ and the church as the greatest prophet of all time. He stood on the cusp of God's dealings with his people in the Old Testament and the New Covenant about to be revealed in Jesus. John 1:29-36 tells us that John the Baptist called Israel and the world to recognize Jesus as "the Christ"—the Savior ("Lamb of God") and Lord ("Son of God"). John baptized Jesus at the inauguration of Jesus' public ministry and John submitted his own ministry and following to the true King.

1. Following John's arrest and imprisonment by Herod, John sent some of his followers to ask a question of Jesus. What was this question (vv. 2-3), and what might have motivated it?

   Has there been a moment when you questioned the identity of Jesus? What was happening in your life at that time?

2. How did Jesus respond to John's question (vv. 4-6), and what do you think he was trying to communicate?

3. Notice how Jesus describes what will happen when the kingdom of God comes upon humans (v. 5). Where or how have you experienced the effect of the kingdom in your own life?

4. In spite of the doubts or struggles John may have had, what does Jesus say about John's stature (v. 11)?

5. Jesus says that John's testimony marks the start of the advance of the kingdom and that those who follow after will be even greater than he was. Notice the provocative word— "forceful"—Jesus uses to describe the character and commitment of those who take hold of the kingdom (v. 12). How does this express itself in your life?

6. What questions or issues does this passage raise for you?

"IT IS PRECISELY WHEN EVERY EARTHLY HOPE HAS BEEN EXPLORED AND FOUND WANTING, . . . WHEN IN THE SHIVERING COLD THE LAST [STICK OF WOOD] HAS BEEN THROWN ON THE FIRE . . . THAT CHRIST'S HAND REACHES OUT, SURE AND FIRM. THEN CHRIST'S WORDS BRING THEIR INEXPRESSIBLE COMFORT, THEN HIS LIGHT SHINES BRIGHTEST, ABOLISHING THE DARKNESS FOREVER. SO FINDING IN EVERYTHING ONLY DECEPTION AND NOTHINGNESS, THE SOUL IS CONSTRAINED TO [TURN] TO GOD HIMSELF AND TO REST CONTENT WITH HIM."

Malcolm Muggeridge, *The End of Christendom*

Reading: Adopters of the Kingdom of God

In his book *The Divine Conspiracy,* Dallas Willard shares a story from his youth that is immensely helpful in understanding the importance of our study of the kingdom of God and its relationship to the role of Christian leaders.

> As a child, I lived in an area of southern Missouri where electricity was available only in the form of lightening. We had more of that than we could use. But in my senior year of high school the Rural Electrification Administration extended its lines into the area where we lived, and electrical power became available to households and farms. When those lines came by our farm, a very different way of living presented itself. Our relationships to fundamental aspects of life—daylight and dark, hot and cold, clean and dirty, work and leisure, preparing food and serving it—could then be vastly changed for the better. But we still had to believe in the electricity and its arrangements, understand them, and take the practical steps involved in *relying* on it.

Some people, of course, immediately saw the potential benefits and took steps to access them. But, for others, the transition to the new world came a lot more slowly or not at all.

> Those farmers . . . in effect, heard the message: "Repent, for electricity is at hand." Repent, or turn from their kerosene lamps and lanterns, their iceboxes and cellars, their scrubboards and rug beaters, their woman-powered sewing machines and their radios with dry-cell batteries. The power that could make their lives far better was right there near them where, by making relatively simple

arrangements, they could utilize it. Strangely, a few did not accept it. They did not "enter the kingdom of electricity." Some just didn't want to change. Others could not afford it, or so they thought.[1]

What does this dichotomy have to say about the perspective of leaders and the part they play in helping others make changes needed to enter the new kingdom that Christ brings? Perhaps a lesson from the social sciences will make this even clearer.

THE DIFFUSION OF KINGDOMS

For decades, sociologists have been fascinated by the patterns of social and technological changes. The classic book in the field is a 1962 study by Everett Rogers titled *The Diffusion of Innovations.* In this work Rogers contends that massive change is always aided by a small group of people—a bare 13 percent of the population—whom he classifies as "early adopters." These are people who catch on early to the potential of an innovation. Long before there is a visible groundswell for adopting the innovation, these "social leaders" see its implications and begin to arrange their lives accordingly. In effect, they pay to have the electrical wire strung into their homes and businesses. Before the neon signs appear, they make the changes required to adapt to the coming world.

In a sense, leading disciples may be thought of as early adopters of the kingdom of God. They are not natives of the kingdom. By grace, however, they are awakened to the possibilities created by the fact that God's presence and power is truly "at hand" or "near"—that is, God's power is *available* to those who cooperate with him.

The Bible presents a luminous display of what God does through such persons. Noah strenuously adapted to the reality of God's coming judgment, even though no one else did. Moses accepted the "new" God who was determined to set his people free from slavery, even though Pharaoh and most of the Egyptians and Hebrews refused to believe it. Samuel adapted to the new kind of king God would raise up for his people, eventually anointing a scrawny shepherd boy named David rather than the more likely candidates for the throne. Nehemiah made stunning arrangements to cooperate with God's call to rebuild Jerusalem, which virtually everyone else had given up for lost. Every one of these leaders recognized (adopted) and relied on (adapted to) the presence and power of a God who would do what seemed impractical or impossible.

The stories of William Wilberforce, Carl and Hud (recounted in chap. 6) are evidence that this pattern continues. We see it in the work of Chuck Colson's Prison Fellowship, renewing the lives of inmates around the world in a way that few believed possible. We encounter it in the story of "Mama Maggie" Gobran, a former college professor, who, in response to God's inbreaking vision, has brought hope and health to thousands of kids living in the garbage dumps of Cairo, Egypt. When we have the eyes to see, we find that God gives us a vision of what he can do with disciples willing to respond to his kingdom's call.

Nowhere, however, is this pattern more vivid than in the New Testament. In describing the beginning of Jesus' public ministry, Mark says: "Jesus went into Galilee, proclaiming the good news of God. 'The time has come,' he said. 'The kingdom of God is near. Repent and believe the good news!' " (Mark 1:14-15). In other words, "Something *new* is happening.

Adapt yourself to it!" Jesus' announcement of the kingdom was a declaration that with his coming the ultimate power and presence of the invisible God had strung a bezillion-watt cable into human life. For those willing to attach themselves to him, life would begin to change at every conceivable level.

Matthew's Gospel pictures for us the first people who began to adopt and adapt to this great innovation: "As Jesus was walking beside the Sea of Galilee, he saw two brothers, Simon called Peter and his brother Andrew. They were casting a net into the lake, for they were fishermen. 'Come, follow me,' Jesus said, 'and I will make you fishers of men.' At once they left their nets and followed him" (Matthew 4:18-20).

LEADERSHIP REQUIRES A KINGDOM CONCEPT

Drawing from these lessons, it is clear that Christian leaders must have a clarifying concept of "ultimate reality"—of the world as it really is and will be. Jesus says that what apparently worked in the former world (pre-Jesus) will not work in the world that is breaking through. And people determined to be part of the most influential forces in heaven and earth will grasp and respond to the new. Jesus put it this way: "From the days of John the Baptist until now, the kingdom of heaven has been forcefully advancing, and forceful [people]"—that is, leaders—"lay hold of it" (Matthew 11:12).

A secular comparison perhaps makes the point clearer. As Thomas Friedman points out in his book *The World Is Flat,* effective leaders in the manufacturing, technology and service industries today grasp the evolving nature of the global marketplace. They understand that the parochial perspectives that might have allowed them to make profits in the past will no longer work in the future. They therefore forcefully lay hold of the means of adapting to the new world.

Christian leaders must be forceful in this sense too. Throughout the Gospels, Jesus declared the existence of an ultimate King and kingdom whose rule and ways are preeminently good and will finally prevail. Our failure to adapt will be our loss. As Dallas Willard maintains, being Jesus' disciple may seem costly, but the cost of nondiscipleship is much greater. It is like living in a rural community that fails to adapt to the existence of electricity. We may have plenty of neighbors who do likewise, but ultimately the way of life we have known will be surpassed by the new. And we will be proven fools for not adapting to the in-breaking reality that revolutionizes life.

Christian leaders are intent on understanding the nature and living by the principles of the kingdom of God. Questions that drive them are, What is the nature of this kingdom, and how do I work for its advancement? In helping to answer these questions, the Bible uses several key concepts that are absolutely central to a Christian leader's vision.

The kingdom of God comprises much more than the church. Pastors need to repent of the notion that God cares primarily for what happens in church buildings. Why? Because Jesus,

> "I HAVE THE AUDACITY TO BELIEVE THAT PEOPLE EVERYWHERE CAN HAVE THREE MEALS A DAY FOR THEIR BODIES, EDUCATION AND CULTURE FOR THEIR MINDS, AND DIGNITY, EQUALITY, AND FREEDOM FOR THEIR SPIRITS. I BELIEVE THAT WHAT SELF-CENTERED MEN HAVE TORN DOWN, OTHER-CENTERED MEN CAN BUILD UP."
>
> Martin Luther King Jr., *Strength to Love*

our model leader, did not put his focus there. Sadly, we often live as if Jesus said, "For God so loved the church that he sent his only begotten Son" (see John 3:16). But this isn't so. Jesus loves his church. But his vision for "the world" is broader than the church. Christ gave his beloved, the church, the special mission of extending God's kingdom (i.e., the way and will of God) "into all the world" (Mark 16:15). God's primary concern for what happens underneath a steeple is the way it equips us to live when we are in our home, the workplace, school and other institutions. Notice how relatively little time Jesus spends teaching in synagogues or the temple courts, and how much more he interacts with people in their homes or villages.

The kingdom of God is focused on the radical renewal of life. Jesus tells us that the King aims to restore the whole world to the state of health and wholeness with which it began. Jesus said, "The Son of Man came to seek and to save what was lost" (Luke 19:10). "I have come that they may have life, and have it to the full" (John 10:10). God is utterly committed to straightening out what has gone wrong with creation and is actively moving against everything that keeps it broken.

Sometimes this work is spoken of in terms of *healing.*

Jesus went through all the towns and villages, teaching in their synagogues, preaching the good news of the kingdom, and healing every disease and sickness. (Matthew 9:35)

He sent them out to preach the kingdom of God and to heal the sick. (Luke 9:2)

[Jesus] welcomed them and spoke to them about the kingdom of God, and healed those who needed healing. (Luke 9:11)

Heal the sick who are there and tell them, "The kingdom of God is near you." (Luke 10:9)

Other times, the work of the kingdom is spoken in terms of *driving out evil*—in other words, that which opposes God's benevolent reign. Jesus said, "If I drive out demons by the Spirit of God, then the kingdom of God has come upon you" (Matthew 12:28; see also Luke 11:20).

Christian leaders therefore aren't primarily interested in starting or governing organizations—whether in the church or in society. They aren't focused on running committees or developing action plans (as important as these might be). At core, Christian leaders have set their hearts on the complete renewal of human life and this world that God has made. In other words, they may be involved with church hospitality or small groups, but their fundamental aim isn't adding more members to the church's rolls. It is, instead, cooperating with God's aim to heal the estrangement between God and humans and between one person and another. Christian leaders may volunteer in a community hunger program or some other charitable effort, but their commitment is more than merely making society a little bit kinder and gentler. They are cooperating with God in expelling the evil that degrades the creatures and creation God dearly loves. They may practice recycling or support the local humane society, but their ultimate interest is not simply slowing global warming or reducing the number of unwanted pets. It is, instead, restoring the careful stewardship of the Earth, mandated by God at creation (Gen 1—2). In all these ways and many more, Christian leaders are devoted to doing their part in advancing the King's plan to reconcile relationships, to establish peace and justice, to completely redeem and renew life at every level.

The kingdom of God determines the success of human endeavors. Christian leaders, as we've described, are committed to some very ambitious outcomes. Nonetheless, they remain clear about the Source of the renovation they seek. In the Old Testament we read:

> Yours, O Lord, is the greatness and
>   the power
> and the glory and the majesty and the
>   splendor,
> for everything in heaven and earth is
>   yours.
> Yours, O Lord, is the kingdom;
>   you are exalted as head over all.
>   (1 Chronicles 29:11)

The Lord established the kingdom under [King Jehoshaphat's] control; and all Judah brought gifts to Jehoshaphat, so that he had great wealth and honor.

And the kingdom of Jehoshaphat was at peace, for his God had given him rest on every side. (2 Chronicles 17:5; 20:30)

Christian leaders don't simply nod in God's direction as they embrace a human enterprise. They understand that if their work is to endure, it will be because it is aligned with God's will. Their leadership is marked by an earnest seeking of God's leading. They devote themselves and their teams to extended amounts of prayer. They remain open to changing course as God leads. They don't depend on human ingenuity but the divine genius. As Jesus himself modeled for his leading disciples, the consistent exclamation of the Christian leader's life is "your kingdom come . . . your will be done" (Matthew 6:10; see also Matthew 26:42).

The kingdom grows organically, not mechanically. Worldly conceptions of leadership often promote command and control, systems and structures, production schedules and other management mechanisms. There certainly is a place for careful attention to organizational practices. At the heart, however, Christian leaders understand that the kingdom of God often defies popular ideas of management.

- Kingdom leaders focus on planting small seeds. Jesus once asked: "What shall we say the kingdom of God is like, or what parable shall we use to describe it? It is like a mustard seed, which is the smallest seed you plant in the ground. Yet when planted, it grows and becomes the largest of all garden plants, with such big branches that the birds of the air can perch in its shade" (Mark 4:30-32).

Christian leaders care, of course, about the large outcome. They know, however, that the most far-reaching changes happen because of small, focused investments made with very good "seeds." For this reason they are less concerned with "doing things right" and more with "doing right things." They live with a persevering hope that perhaps the next good investment will create a tipping point that brings about desired change.

- Kingdom leaders focus on relationships.

As Jesus himself did, they put extraordinary amounts of energy into caring for and mentoring individuals. They believe that focusing on people generates outcomes much better than obsessing about programs and production. As Reggie McNeal said to me (Dan), Christian leaders are more concerned with "getting people done through work" than with "getting work done through people." They believe that the small acts of integrity and love by which they conduct their leadership matter more than the apparent results. They know that their greatest legacy will not be the towering institutions they leave behind but the tremendous individuals who carry on the witness and work of God's kingdom.

- Kingdom leaders trust God for the harvest. Christian leaders understand that not every seed they plant will take root and flourish. They focus more on sowing faithfully than on reaping fanatically. They expect a certain amount of apparent failure. Because Jesus teaches them that weeds often grow up alongside and in competition with good wheat, they don't expect perfection in people or in the ministries they lead. They also understand that God may be at work invisibly and on a schedule that is wiser than theirs. Along with the apostle Paul, they grasp that it is their job to plant and to water as best they can, but God makes the seed grow (1 Corinthians 3:6) and establishes the time for the great harvest.

LEADERSHIP REQUIRES A KINGDOM CHANGE

Though they hold this relaxed focus, Christian leaders are not passive. They know that the kingdom is not about fine-tuning the way things are. Just as entering into the "kingdom of electricity" requires widespread changes, Christian leaders understand that living in the kingdom of God necessitates dramatic change in the way humans approach life. They know that Jesus consistently tied his teaching about the kingdom to a call to repent (Mark 1:14-15).

When you want to enter into God's kingdom, Jesus said, you will have to drop some of your familiar nets (Mark 1:18). You will need to turn around, sacrificing some of your former commitments (Luke 9:59-60). You will have to change your well-established orientation (Matthew 18:3). You will need to be born again (John 3:3), to discard the old wineskins in favor of the new (Luke 5:37-38), to quit depending on the securities that formerly defined you (Luke 18:24-25). Entering the kingdom of God requires handling money, appetites, enemies and priorities in a way that differs from the kingdom of this darkened world.

Kingdom leaders are people who understand that while "Jesus Christ is the same yesterday and today and forever" (Hebrews 13:8), the rest of us must *change!* Leaders must, of course, be careful not to make change for change's sake or in order to leave their mark on everything. (This happens far too often!) Nonetheless, Christian leaders will frequently

> "A FOREIGN VISITOR ONCE MADE THIS COMMENT ABOUT U.S. CHURCHES: 'YOU AMERICANS ARE SO CONCERNED ABOUT BEING HAPPY, AS IF OUR KINGDOMS WERE THE FOCAL POINT OF GOD'S DESIGNS RATHER THAN GOD'S KINGDOM THE FOCAL POINT OF OURS.'"
>
> Evelyn Bence, *Christianity Today*

ask, "What do we need to alter to cooperate with what God is doing here? Have we slipped into a worldly mindset in the way we're approaching this issue (or person)? What do we need to let go or take hold of in order to better adapt to the vision and values of the kingdom of God?"

LEADERSHIP REQUIRES A KINGDOM COMMITMENT

Commitment to the kingdom can be difficult. Like discipleship, kingdom leadership always costs something. It takes time and energy. It results in criticism and conflict. It can seem painstakingly slow or confusing at times. Jesus said however: "The kingdom of heaven is like treasure hidden in a field. When a man found it, he hid it again, and then in his joy went and sold all he had and bought that field. Again, the kingdom of heaven is like a merchant looking for fine pearls. When he found one of great value, he went away and sold everything he had and bought it" (Matthew 13:44-46).

Being a part of God's kingdom is worth the price, no matter how expensive. Being part of the genuine transformation of even one soul; dedicating your life to building up something that will surely outlast every human institution; rubbing shoulders with Jesus Christ in the yoke that pulls people toward wholeness; knowing God's presence and power moving in and through you; being a cherished officer in the company of saints whose membership and influence spans all races, genders and times; standing at last in front of the great Innovator, the ultimate Leader and hearing him say, "Well done!" is quite simply the greatest prize of Christian leadership. It is well worth the cost. "I tell you the truth," Jesus once said to his leading disciples, "no one who has left [anything] for the sake of the kingdom of God will fail to receive many times as much in this age and, in the age to come, eternal life" (Luke 18:29-30).

The truth is, the kingdom of God's divine power is at hand. It is nearer to us than our own heartbeat. He is intent on lighting up the whole world and redeeming every willing life from darkness. He is transforming a planet of shadowed shacks into a city of radiant light (Revelation 21:1-5; 22:5). And the wonder is that we Christian leaders get to play a part in the renewal.

---

[1]Dallas Willard, *The Divine Conspiracy* (SanFrancisco: HarperSanFrancisco, 1998), pp. 30-31.

Leadership Exercise: Assessing Your Kingdom Vision

1. Where do you see evidence in yourself or others that the kingdom of God has been reduced to what happens within the church?

2. Think for a moment about the way you have tended to approach leadership. Complete the following sentence: Those who know me best would likely say that my leadership is motivated mainly by the passion:

   - to be in charge or advance my standing in some way
   - to hold committee meetings
   - to organize information, resources, people or activities
   - to renew the quality of life in some corner of the earth
   - other _____

   If you were to put the mission of the ministry team or organization you lead in terms of radical renewal (e.g., healing some ill or driving out some evil), how would you describe it?

3. What specific disciplines or practices do you exercise to ensure that your leadership is grounded in the principle that "the King and his kingdom determines the success of human endeavors"? If this principle is not currently in force, when and where will you do this?

4. If it is true that the kingdom grows organically (not mechanically), then

   - What are some small "seeds" you are (or could be) planting that could one day become large trees?

   - Where do you see yourself focused on relationships? Who are the specific people in whom you are (or could be) carefully planting right now? List them.

- On a scale of 1-10 (1 = "not at all" and 10 = "completely"), how would you rate your trust in God for a harvest in the work you are leading?

  Not at All   1   2   3   4   5   6   7   8   9   10   Completely

What makes this easy or hard for you?

5. Entering more fully into the kingdom of God requires repentance. Reflect on the meaning of this for you or the leadership team you work with.
   - What do I (we) need to alter to cooperate with what God wants to do here?
   - Where have I (we) slipped into a worldly mindset in the way I'm (we're) approaching the people or issues we face?
   - What do I (we) need to let go or take hold of for God's kingdom to more fully come through my (our) leadership?

6. As you would do for any other significant investment, do a simple cost-benefit analysis on your involvement in the kingdom's work.

              Cost   Benefit

7. Does the reading convict, challenge or comfort you? Why?

Going Deeper

Willard, Dallas. *The Divine Conspiracy*. San Francisco: HarperSanFrancisco, 1998.

Evans, Tony. *The Kingdom Agenda: What a Way to Live*. Chicago: Moody Publishers, 2006.

Rogers, Mike C., and Claude V. King, *The Kingdom Agenda: Experiencing God in Your Workplace*. Nashville: Lifeway Press, 1997.

9 / Helping Others See

LOOKING AHEAD

Memory Verse: Proverbs 29:18
Bible Study: Matthew 10:5-31
Reading: The Passion and Practices of Visionary Leadership
Leadership Exercise: Forming a Vision-Building Plan

 Core Truth

What is the essence of visionary leadership from a Christian perspective?

Visionary leadership is the art of picturing God's preferred future for people in terms that inspire their souls and invigorate their wills. It also helps people discern and discipline themselves to the specific principles and practices God uses to transform that dream into reality.

1. Identify key words or phrases in the question and answer above, and state their meaning in your own words.

2. Restate the core truth in your own words.

3. What questions or issues does the core truth raise for you?

Memory Verse Study Guide

Copy the entire text here:

Memory Verse: Proverbs 29:18

Leadership is the art of multiplying influence through *other* people. As important as it is to have our *own* vision of the kingdom, we aren't truly *leading* until we are helping others catch and live by God's vision. Our memory verse makes clear why this is so crucial.

1. *Putting it in context.* The book of Proverbs has been traditionally viewed as an anthology of the wisdom of King Solomon of Israel, a well-seasoned leader himself. Read the list of leadership maxims in Proverbs 29:1-17. What are a few of the transferable principles of leadership you notice there?

2. In the KJV of the memory verse reads: "Where there is no vision, the people perish: but he that keepeth the law, happy is he." Describe the importance Solomon attaches to a people having a "vision." (What does he say happens when there is no vision?)

3. The NAB translation of this verse says that without a vision, "the people become demoralized." How can a lack of vision be demoralizing?

4. The NIV says that without a vision "the people cast off restraint." What's the connection between having a clear vision and demonstrating restraint?

5. Solomon implies that when a people have a clear vision from God, they take action to "keep the law" (i.e., fulfill God's intentions), and this in turn leads to happiness. When have you seen vision lead to action and greater happiness among a group of people?

Inductive Bible Study Guide

Bible Study: Matthew 10:5-31

The passage in this study pictures how Jesus, the ultimate leader, equips and sends the Twelve to do the work he has called them to do. The text helps us see that being a visionary leader requires giving people more than a general picture of the need to be addressed or the outcome desired. It also means helping them see the specific, practical path they'll use in pursuing the vision.

1. What does Jesus say about the *target audience* that the Twelve are to pursue (vv. 5-6)?

2. What *specific message* are the disciples asked to convey wherever they go (v. 7)?

> "PEOPLE DO NOT FOLLOW PROGRAMS, BUT LEADERS WHO INSPIRE THEM. THEY ACT WHEN A VISION STIRS IN THEM A RECKLESS HOPE OF SOMETHING GREATER THAN THEMSELVES, HOPE OF FULFILLMENT THEY NEVER BEFORE DARED TO ASPIRE TO. AND HOPE IS PASSED FROM PERSON TO PERSON. . . . HOPE BURSTS INTO FLAME WHEN LEADERS BEGIN TO ACT."

3. What *practical acts* does Jesus call them to perform in order to incarnate that message (v. 8)?

4. What *resource and relationship-building plan* does Jesus give them to supply their needs (vv. 9-12)?

> John White, *Excellence in Leadership*

5. What are some of the *realistic expectations* Jesus sets concerning the challenges the Twelve will face (vv. 13-15, 17-18)?

6. What *guidelines for handling adversity* does Jesus give to his disciples? In other words, what truths, assurances or strategies are they supposed to hang onto when things get rough (vv. 14-16, 19-31)?

7. In summary, how does Jesus model visionary leadership?

8. What questions or issues does this passage raise for you?

👓 Reading: The Passion and Practices of Visionary Leadership

If God kept files on human history, one of the fattest would have to be labeled "Blindness." It would include millions of stories that illustrate the sometimes comical and often tragic capacity of humans to miss the possibilities before them, and to do so with an almost amazing self-assurance.

For instance, an American authority once declared that the introduction of the railroad would require the construction of many insane asylums! He was convinced that people would be driven positively mad with terror at the sight of locomotives rushing by. In 1870, a speaker addressing an assembly of Indiana Methodists offered a different perspective on transportation: "I believe we are coming into a time of great inventions . . . when men will fly through the air like birds." "That's heresy!" exclaimed the presiding bishop. "God has reserved flight for the angels!" Bishop Wright then went home and told his two sons, Wilbur and Orville, how things would always be!

In 1899, Charles Duell, director of the U.S. Patent Office, petitioned the president of the United States to close his department, saying, "Everything that can be invented has been invented." In 1923, Robert Millikan, a Nobel Prize winner in physics, declared, "There is no likelihood man can ever tap the power of the atom."

Here's one of our favorites. Following the phenomenal success of the Beatles, John Lennon built a beautiful home for his mother near the cliffs of Dover. Over the mantel Lennon placed a polished brass plaque engraved with the words he'd heard from his mother almost daily while growing up: "Playing the guitar and singing is just fine, John; but you'll never be able to make a living doing it."

THE ROLE AND RIPPLES OF THE IMPOSSIBLE DREAMER

Where would we be without the visionaries of this world? Where would we be without those who were willing to stand up to all the reasons why something can't be done, and who dared to say "Let's get it done"? The answer, as King Solomon declares in Proverbs 29:18, is that we would "perish" (KJV). Life as God intended it to be—the life of the kingdom—withers when there is no vision. Those who have a specific vision of a future good lead the changes that enable people to cross vast distances, heal the sick and compose music that inspires the human soul.

Paraphrasing a work by George Bernard Shaw, Robert F. Kennedy Jr. declared, "Some people see things as they are and say why? I dream things that never were and say *why not?*"[1] Leading disciples are dreamers like this. They are compelled by a vision of a preferred future God has shown them—some specific good, some manifestation of the kingdom's life—that will not become real without people giving themselves to it. Maybe that preferred future is a change in their family or church. Perhaps it is a new reality in their organization or workplace. Maybe it is a yet-unrealized possibility for their neighborhood or community. Whatever the context, it is the Christian leader's persistent articulation of this vision that helps lift people out of the natural lethargy that keeps them trapped in the perishing world.

Common Characteristics of Godly Visions

The Bible is chock-full of instances when God planted such pictures of a preferred future into the minds of those he wanted to accomplish his purposes. When we study these biblical stories closely, several common characteristics seem to mark these godly visions.

1. Godly visions depict an outcome that may seem outrageous given present reality. Imagine how these biblical characters must have felt when God first challenged them: *"Noah,* you're going to build a gigantic ark in the middle of dry land, and this boat will save you from the coming flood." *"Sarah,* I know you are an old woman, but out of your womb I am going to birth a new nation." *"Joseph,* don't let this prison discourage you; you're going to be Pharaoh's righthand man." *"Moses,* I know you are afraid of public speaking, but I will use you to convince Pharaoh to let my people go." *"Nehemiah,* the ruined city of Jerusalem will be rebuilt under your direction." *"Mary,* you're going to bear and raise the Savior of the world." *"Saul,* as a Christian, you will spread my gospel to the ends of the earth." Each of these visions was outrageous. Yet, as history demonstrates, these vi-

> "EACH TIME A [PERSON] STANDS UP FOR AN IDEAL, OR ACTS TO IMPROVE THE LOT OF OTHERS, OR STRIKES OUT AGAINST INJUSTICE, HE SENDS FORTH A TINY RIPPLE OF HOPE, AND CROSSING EACH OTHER FROM A MILLION DIFFERENT CENTERS OF ENERGY AND DARING, THOSE RIPPLES BUILD A CURRENT THAT CAN SWEEP DOWN THE MIGHTIEST WALLS OF OPPRESSION AND RESISTANCE."
>
> Robert F. Kennedy Jr., from an address given to South African young people on their Day of Affirmation, 1966

sions led to steps of faithfulness and stunning outcomes.

2. Visions bring glory to God and draw people to him. In their bestselling book *Built to Last,* Stanford Business School professors Jim Collins and Jerry I. Porras contend that part of what sets truly great organizations apart from merely good ones is their willingness to set BHAGs—"Big Hairy Audacious Goals." These goals are so audacious that they energize the ambitions of people in a way that ordinary goals can't. In the same way, the big, hairy, audacious visions of God also have a way of inspiring great effort from those who pursue them. However, these visions differ from the world's approach to goal-setting in two important ways.

First, godly visions seek outcomes that are not possible without God's input. In this sense, then, they are not BHAGs but GSGs—"God-sized Goals." They may involve strenuous human involvement, but they require God-sized action to come to pass. Those who have such visions are clear that unless the Lord is involved, their work is in vain (see Psalm 127:1). They say, "We've got to give this effort our absolute best, but if God doesn't work here, we'll never see this vision realized." The apostle Paul voiced this clearly at a time when the Corinthians were focusing too much on human efforts: "What, after all, is Apollos? And what is Paul? Only servants, through whom you came to believe—as the Lord has assigned to each his task. I planted the seed, Apollos watered it, but God made it grow. So neither he who plants nor he who waters is anything, but only God, who makes things grow" (1 Corinthians 3:5-7).

Second, a vision's fulfillment is not about the elevation of individuals and institutions but the exaltation of God. Jesus urged this kind of holy ambition when he said, "Let your light shine before men, that they may see your good deeds and praise to your Father in heaven" (Matthew 5:16). And Paul said, "We have this treasure in jars of clay to show that this all-surpassing power is from God and not from us" (2 Corinthians 4:7). For God, says Paul, "is able to do immeasurably more than all we ask or imagine, according to his power that is at work within us" (Ephesians 3:20).

3. Godly visions display the character and desires of God. Many people in the arts or politics have visions. But a *godly* vision expresses the character of the King and the quality of his kingdom as revealed in the Bible. Godly visions display God's heart to people—his nature as Savior, Redeemer, Shepherd, Refiner, Planter, and Resurrector of life. To encounter the vision, then, is to meet the Giver behind the vision.

4. Godly visions become contagious. Evidence that a vision truly is from God is that it is adopted by many other faithful people. Abraham's vision that God would bless the nations through his family (Genesis 12:1-5) became the dream of thousands. The Samaritan woman's vision of finding streams of living water through Jesus became the dream of her entire village (John 4:28-30; 39-41). Peter's vision of forming an international community of disciples became the dream of the worldwide church (Acts 1:8; 2:40-47).

TRANSLATING MISSION INTO VISION

If you wish to be a Christian leader, the first question to ask is, What is the vision God has given to me? In answering that question, it is important to recognize the difference between *vision* and *mission*. Rowland Forman explains:

> Contrary to a widely held misconception, vision and mission are not synonymous. *Mission* is a broad-based description of WHY you exist—your purpose for being. It defines the outer parameters of acceptable activity. *Vision* is much more specific; it details the WHAT—the particular direction you will pursue within the broad framework of your mission. Vision provides focus. To use a sports analogy, mission is the *stadium* in which you will play; vision identifies the *sport* to be played within the stadium. Vision is a specific, detailed, customized, distinctive . . . notion of what you are seeking to do to create a particular outcome.[2]

Maybe a specific example will help. The mission of our (Dan and Greg's) church, Christ Church of Oak Brook, is "to gather communities of disciples who worship, grow, and serve and go into all the world as witnesses of the life-changing love of Jesus Christ." This is the "stadium," the large circle or environment in which we labor. If you ask us why we exist, we answer that it is to form communities of disciples who both experience Christ's love and express it to the world. This is our enduring purpose.

But Christ Church of Oak Brook also has a very specific *vision:* "To help 2,500 people experience the joy and significance of life-trans-forming, outreach-oriented small group community in the next three years." This is the particular "sport" we are playing in our mission stadium right now. We're convinced that if we can get a large percentage of our congregation involved in small group communities that are reaching out in love and service to their neighbors, it will profoundly advance our overall mission. This vision isn't just words. It lives in widescreen, high-definition, 3-D format for us.

We picture hundreds of smaller "communities of disciples" meeting in homes, coffee shops and office buildings all over our region. There, people share their honest questions, their true longings, their pain and pleasures. They use a simple curriculum or just the Bible to examine life through the lens of God's Word, and as they do that they begin to see life and a creative path in front of them more clearly. They show up at the hospital when one of their group is sick and at the party when there's something to celebrate. They pray for and encourage each other in facing the sin or struggles of life. Slowly, each person begins to look a bit more like Jesus.

These small groups of disciples start asking, How can we be a greater blessing in this neighborhood, in this town? What need could we address together? One group might befriend an elderly man who's living alone in their neighborhood. Another adopts a local elementary school. Still others take on clean-up projects or raise money to meet a need the town council hasn't been able to fund. One group starts doing yard work and delivering groceries once a month to a single mom struggling to make ends meet. Ideas and practical acts of service multiply.

As these little platoons build authentic connections with people in their neighborhoods and address real needs within their sphere of influence, they witness to Christ's love. They start being, as Robert Lewis suggests, the living proof of the spoken truth that Jesus changes lives. People who had been resistant to religion or who could never see themselves going to church are attracted to what they see in these people. Spiritual conversations start to bubble up naturally. Some of these observers join one of the neighborhood groups or dare to explore a ministry offered inside the church building.

> "FAITH IS BEING SURE OF WHAT WE HOPE FOR AND CERTAIN OF WHAT WE DO NOT SEE."
>
> Hebrews 11:1

As people become part of this movement, they start talking about how they feel much greater joy and significance in their spiritual life than when they merely sat and soaked in a church building. Our large church becomes an amazingly personal and life-impacting community. By the hundreds, people are now regularly inviting others to come and experience the blessing they have experienced. People just can't get over the wonder of God's grace.

This is the vision God has given Christ Church of Oak Brook. This preferred future inspires our leadership team and invigorates us to do what is required to help this dream become reality.

What is the specific vision God has formed, or may be trying to form, in you (or those you lead)? Can you describe in Technicolor what you see happening as the dream morphs into three-dimensional life? When you describe this vision to others, does it make anyone else's heart stir with a passion to see it happen?

Translating Vision into Strategy & Tactics

To recap, your mission is the *why* of your organization or group. Your vision is the *what*. Having these two things well-defined enables you to focus on a third key dimension of visionary leadership: the *how*—the specific strategy you'll pursue to cooperate with God in bringing the vision to pass. This is, frankly, a place where many of us who would like to be "visionary" leaders drop the ball. We love the realm of ideas and words. We can imagine all kinds of possibilities. We can clearly see why we're here and what we long to have happen. We have what is called a "delegating" leadership style. Delegating leaders, in effect, say: "I'll tell you how great the need is. I'll dump the responsibility in your lap. You can figure out for yourself how to get the job done."

Until we invest the time and energy needed to assist our teammates in prayerfully charting *how* we're going to get where we want to go, we aren't fully leading. Back to our athletic metaphor: you can have a marvelous stadium (mission) and an articulate passion for the sport (vision), but unless you also have a thoughtful recruiting program, a disciplined training regimen, a specific game plan, a post-game analysis pattern and so on, you are not likely to be successful at the game you love. Visionary leadership requires helping others see not only what game we're playing but how

> "Vision without action is a daydream. Action without vision is a nightmare."
>
> Japanese Proverb

we're going to play it effectively. This is the realm of strategy (and it's identical twin, tactical execution).

The Bible provides us with numerous examples of visionary leaders who devoted tremendous time and energy to translating vision into strategy (and the tactical actions that flow from it). Look at Joseph's strategy for helping Egypt survive a coming famine (Genesis 41:28-36). Check out Jethro's strategy for saving Moses (and Israel) from leadership burnout (Exodus 18). Examine Nehemiah's strategy to rebuild Jerusalem, physically and spiritually (Nehemiah 1—12). We catch a glimpse of Titus's strategy, coached by his mentor Paul, to fulfill his vision of transforming Crete from a community of stubborn "Cretans" into a community of saints (Titus 1—3).

Perhaps no biblical figure provides as exemplary a leadership strategy model for us as Jesus himself. Before requiring his disciples to take on the burden of leadership, Jesus made sure that they knew how they were to do it. One of his favorite means of doing this was by personally using the principles and practices he sought in them. In the familiar story told in John 13:1-17, for example, Jesus calls for his disciples to practice a footwashing style of servant love—but only after modeling the behavior for them. Other times, Jesus gave those he led what Robert Logan calls "Just In Time" training. In other words, he gave them enough guidance to get them *started* and then remained available when they returned for more guidance (Mark 9:25-29). After their initial experiences, the disciples were ready to take notes on Christ's instructions!

The Matthew 10 Bible study earlier in this chapter vividly describes the measures Jesus took to make sure that the Twelve were clear on what they needed to do to translate vision into reality. Jesus sharply defined the *target audience* they were to focus on—the lost sheep of Israel. He clarified the *specific message* they should convey—that the kingdom of heaven was at hand. He described the *practical tactics* to employ to make that message concrete for people—heal, raise, cleanse, drive out. Jesus laid out the *resource plan* by which they'd be able to feed and shelter themselves along the journey. Furthermore, Jesus set *realistic expectations* about how hard the job would be and the kind of opposition the Twelve might face. They couldn't come back to him later and say, "If I had only known what I was getting into." Jesus also gave them helpful *guidelines for handling adversity.* And he laid out the *rewards and benefits* of completing the mission.

Bringing It Home

What can we do to help people see not just the *why* and *what* of our work but also the *how?* Thankfully, we don't have to personally come up with all the answers to this question. One of your principal roles as a Christian leader, however, is to ensure that the important questions do get asked and answered. In addition to the dimensions already discussed, the following questions can help frame a strategic game plan for almost any organization or group.

- What are the top three or four *major changes or initiatives* that need to be undertaken for the vision to be made a reality?
- What are the *forces* working for and against those changes or initiatives? How do we plan to handle the adversity and opposition we may face?
- What leadership *values* and *passions* will help us advance our vision, and how can we magnify them? For example, who are inspiring leaders we could invite to speak to us?
- What sort of *teams or subteams* will we need to patiently build?
- What kind of *skills training* or *leadership coaching* would help our cause?
- What type of organization-wide *communications* or *teaching* could help advance the vision? What stories need telling?
- What specific *experiences* or *special events* can we give people to help them catch the vision more fully for themselves?
- What *additional resources* (people, technology, capital, etc.) can help undergird this effort? Where might these come from?
- What sort of *feedback loops* are needed to give us a reading on how things are going and where correction is needed?
- How and where will we *celebrate progress* toward the fulfillment of our vision so that discouragement doesn't set in?
- What are the three *specific goals* we will pursue in the next six months to help us make progress on the strategic dimensions identified?
- What are the *partnering rhythms* needed to keep our leadership team personally connected and practically focused on our vision and plan?

Haddon Robinson once observed: "We all see the shrouding mists, but leaders have seen the city. Leaders glimpse what others may not see and are captured by it. That's why they risk everything to reach the city."[3] That's why they also invest so much thought and energy helping other people see those distant ramparts and the path that leads to them. May God bless you as you and your colleagues make this journey.

---

[1]http://en.wikiquote.org/wiki/Robert_F._Kennedy.

[2]Rowland Forman (statement made during the Center for Church-Based Training One-Day Seminar, Naperville, Ill., 2002).

[3]Haddon Robinson, foreword to *Developing a Vision for Ministry in the 21st Century,* by Aubrey Malfurs (Grand Rapids: Baker Books, 1992).

Leadership Exercise: Forming a Vision-Building Plan

Dr. Aubrey Malphurs suggests some helpful vision-development disciplines to which we've added some thoughts of our own.[4] They are offered for you to practice personally or to use with a leadership team.

1. Pray for God's vision.

   • Set aside some time this week to pray for the implanting or refining of the vision God has for you and your leadership team. Make this a regular part of your prayer pattern.

   Creator God, Light of the World, Fire-bringing Spirit, grant me (us) the wisdom to see the needs you see and the mind to think and feel about them as you do. . . . Fill my (our) imagination with a picture of what you desire to bring into being to address those needs. . . . Give me (us) eyes to see the people you want to involve as partners in fulfilling your vision.

   • What thoughts, images and people come to mind during these prayer times, or what people come into your life during this season of prayer?

Specific Needs Possible	Approaches	Potential Partners

2. Think God-sized.

   • What could I reasonably accomplish in the need area(s) identified if I acted on my own?

   • What involvement of God (and other people he connects me with) would it take to bring this to pass? (Read Ephesians 3:14-21.)

   • Who do I know who thinks big or who gives attention to the crucial small investments needed for leadership? List the names of people you could consult for perspective and wisdom.

3. Write about the dream.

   • Record in a journal or notebook what God impresses on you as you pray, reflect and research. Is there a metaphor or image that helps create a mental picture? Collect samples of vision statements you find elsewhere.

- In simple but vivid terms, write the vision God has given you to date.

4. Question the vision.

- Is the dream *clear?* Share the vision with several people and ask them to articulate it back to you. If they can't, refine the statement.

- Is the vision *challenging* or *inspiring?* Ask a variety of people to tell you, honestly, what they feel or think when you articulate the dream.

- Is the vision *visual?* What do you and others "see" when the vision is communicated? What's the three-dimensional picture?

- Is the dream *achievable?* Is it the right blend of realism and faith in God's extraordinary power?

- Is the vision *life-relevant?* Ask others to tell you what impact the achievement of this dream might have on real people.

5. Begin to define or refine your strategy.

- Take another look at the questions posed in the "Bringing It Home" section of the Reading (pp. 130-31). What are two or three questions on that strategic questions list that it might be important to answer sooner rather than later?

- These questions are the most timely ones for me because:

---

[4]Aubrey Malphurs, *Developing a Vision for Ministry in the 21st Century* (Grand Rapids: Baker Books, 1992), pp. 239-41.

Part Four

The Shaping of a Leader

Whether it is Christian ministry, the business world, the political realm or educational institutions, we hear the cry, "Where are the true and courageous leaders today?" There always appears to be a dearth of people who are willing to take responsibility, get out front and lead the way.

It seems there are many more called by God to lead than respond to that call. The primary reason for this "duck and cover" syndrome is that leadership is difficult. We would rather take the easy way. After all, leaders are targets for criticism. It is much easier to tell others what they are doing wrong than to step forward yourself. Leadership requires responsibility, bearing the decision-making burdens and carrying the welfare of others. It demands grace in the presence of ungrateful people and unearthly wisdom to navigate the complexities of varying opinions and degrees of maturity.

Throughout Scripture, from Moses to Peter, reluctance seems to be the mark of godly leadership. Overpowered by God, a potential leader finally concedes—and then faces the pressure cooker. Yet this very pressure is used by God to shape them into the people others will follow.

In this final section, we take a look at the means that God uses to shape a leader's character.

Taming Temptation (chap. 10). Jesus went immediately from his ordination service of baptism to encounter his archenemy Satan. And he later encountered evil in veiled ways, ranging from the pharisaical religious establishment to the corruption of leprosy to the desertion of his disciples. Even so, Christian leaders can count on battles, whether they are the conflicting demands of people's expectations or the lure and enticement of money, sex and power. Yet, though we face the fire, God is faithful to refine us into pure gold.

Conquering Criticism (chap. 11). Jesus was accused of being a "friend of sinners" and "a glutton and drunkard." The Son of God had his critics, and we should not expect anything less. Leaders are public targets. It is as if we have a sign pinned to our backs: "Take your best shot." Criticism is inevitable. We need wisdom and grace from above to sort through it and ask, "Lord, what truth do I need to hear, and what can I let go?" The Lord uses criticism to build into us a generosity of spirit and strength to endure, while guarding against cynicism. For this to happen, we need to stay close to the One who endured the cross for the sake of the joy set before him.

Defeating Discouragement (chap. 12). Leadership is lonely and at times feels a lot like banging your head against the wall. Moses had to deal with the complaining masses who thought that captivity in Egypt looked a lot better than freedom in the wilderness. He had to navigate between the "poor me" syndrome (complaining about what God had gotten him into) and anger (he'd just as soon be done with the ingrates). This is the reality of leadership. How does a leader deal with the inevitable anger or depression that comes with the territory?

10 / Taming Temptation

LOOKING AHEAD

Memory Verse: 1 Peter 5:1-4
Bible Study: 1 Kings 11:1-13
Reading: Facing Temptation as the Beloved of the Father
Leadership Exercise: Naming Our Temptations

 ## Core Truth

What must Christian leaders guard against?

Since the health of the Christian community reflects the health of its leaders, leading disciples are a primary target of the evil one. Satan will attempt to separate leaders from the source of their life, their connection with the living God. When Christian leaders are not grounded firmly in their identity as beloved in Christ, they are particularly susceptible to the lure of money, sex or power to fill the deficit.

1. Identify key words or phrases in the question and answer above, and state their meaning in your own words.

2. Restate the core truth in your own words.

3. What questions or issues does the core truth raise for you?

Memory Verse Study Guide

Copy the entire text here:

Memory Verse: 1 Peter 5:1-4

The apostle Peter addresses the elders (pastors) of the churches who are dispersed throughout Asia Minor (modern-day Turkey—see 1 Peter 1:1). Peter is representative of the New Testament writers who seem to be not nearly as concerned about what leaders do (job description) as they are about the why and way they do it. In our memory verse Peter warns the leaders of the particular pitfalls that they are to avoid.

1. *Putting it in context.* In 1 Peter 5:1, Peter identifies with the elders and states that he is "a witness of Christ's sufferings." How does this phrase connect to the context of 1 Peter 4:12-19?

2. Peter identifies three wrong motives for Christian leadership. Capture in your own words what Peter is calling leaders to turn away from:

   "not because you must" (v. 2)

   "not greedy for money" (v. 2)

   "not lording it over those entrusted to you" (v. 3)

3. Where do the correctives get too close to you for comfort?

4. What corrective does Peter give to combat each of these false motives (v. 3)?

5. According to verse 4, what is the leader's primary motive, which can serve as a purifier of the heart?

Inductive Bible Study Guide

Bible Study: 1 Kings 11:1-13

King Solomon might be considered the saddest character in the entire Bible. He started out so well, had it all and finished in disgrace. Instead of asking for long life, wealth or power at the beginning of his reign as King of Israel, he asked for an understanding mind to discern what was right (1 Kings 3). God rewarded him with the kind of wisdom (see Proverbs) that attracted people from great distances. In addition, Solomon was allowed to do what was forbidden to his father David—build the great temple in Jerusalem, which was considered to be the house of God. His prayer at the dedication of the temple demonstrates his reverence for the one, true God (1 Kings 8:23). And yet his life ended in shame; the allure of foreign wives drew him away from the true God. The tragedy of Solomon should a send holy shudder into the heart of any leader.

1. Take some time to skim through 1 Kings 3—10. What were some of the ways God's favor rested on Solomon?

2. Note the repetition of the promise and warning given to Solomon (1 Kings 3:14; 6:11-13; 9:4-9). Take particular notice of the prayer that Solomon offers at the dedication of the temple starting at 1 Kings 8:22. Then focus on the benediction he pronounces over the people (1 Kings 8:56-61). What did Solomon know about the Lord and his expectations for him and God's people?

3. *Read 1 Kings 11:1-13.* According to 1 Kings 11:1-8, what was it that drew Solomon's heart away from the true God?

What is so alluring about this power?

4. How could someone who had all of Solomon's advantages walk away from what he knew to be right?

5. What do you fear could gain a stronghold in your heart to turn you away from passionate, faithful service to the Lord?

Reading: Facing Temptation as the Beloved of the Father

Christian leader, you have a target on your back. Satan wants to take you out. Though Satan's ultimate ambition is to destroy the One who defeated him on the cross, he will attempt to get at Jesus through us. Addressing his fellow elders, the apostle Peter warns, "Your enemy the devil prowls around like a roaring lion looking for someone to devour" (1 Peter 5:8). By discrediting our character, Satan also discredits Christ and his cause.

THE TEMPTATION OF JESUS IN THE WILDERNESS

We need to know what temptations Satan uses to bring leading disciples down and where we might be most susceptible to his strategy. Thus we turn to the temptation of Jesus in order to acquaint ourselves with the devil's pattern. What did Satan dangle in front of Jesus to separate him from his Father?

Before we examine the specific temptations that Jesus faced, it is vital to observe what immediately preceded the wilderness encounter. In the Synoptic Gospels, all three accounts of Jesus' encounter with Satan are preceded by Jesus' baptism. As Jesus emerged from the Jordan River, the Scriptures say that the Spirit descended in the form of a dove and that then his Father added a special word. In Mark's and Luke's account, the Father's word is personal, "You are my Son, whom I love; with you I am well pleased" (Mark 1:11; Luke 3:22). It is as if the Father is saying, "Son, as I send you into this hostile world, I want you to know more than anything else the special place you have in my heart."

Matthew changes the message slightly but significantly. Instead of a private word to Jesus, Matthew says that the Father spoke to those around Jesus, "This is my Son, whom I love; with him I am well pleased" (Matthew 3:17). This nuance shifts the emphasis to a papa who is busting at the seams with pride over the identity of his son. Like human parents who want to stand up and shout when their children have won an award or scored a winning goal, the Father is saying, "Do you know who this is? This is my Son." It is as if the Father couldn't restrain himself. In *The Message* Eugene Peterson captures the Father's enthusiasm, "This is my son, chosen and marked by my love, delight of my life."

Of all the things the Father could have said at the beginning of his Son's redemptive work, why these words? It is because even Jesus needed to know what he meant to the Father—that he was the apple of his Father's eye. As Jesus stood on the threshold of a public ministry destined for a cross, the Father wanted his Son to know that when life turned bleak the Son remained the Father's beloved. Baptism was Jesus' "coming out" moment; the only place of ultimate safety is to be hidden in the heart of the Father.

THE WILDERNESS EXPERIENCE

Why does the affirmation of Jesus' worth and value to the Father precede Jesus' temptation? Is there a direct connection? Yes. First, the temptations were Satan's assault on Jesus' belief that he is the beloved Son of the Father. Second, Jesus' understanding that he is the Father's beloved was the ground on which he fought the battle.

What is true of Jesus is also true of us. The highest privilege and fundamental reality of a

Christian leader's life is that we have been adopted into the family of God. Jesus, as the unique, eternal Son of the Father, gave his life so that we who were born orphans, separated and at odds with the Father because of our sin, could become the adopted, beloved sons and daughters of God. The apostle Paul says, "For you did not receive a spirit that makes you a slave again to fear, but you have received the Spirit of sonship [through adoption]. And by him we cry, 'Abba, Father' [just like Jesus (see Mark 14:36)]. The Spirit himself testifies with our spirit that we are God's children" (Romans 8:15-16). J. I. Packer says it simply, "What is a Christian? The question can be answered in many ways, but the richest answer I know is that a Christian is one who has God for his Father."[1]

Jesus' temptation reveals that ultimately all temptation is an attempt to drive a wedge between the Father-child relationship. Consequently, if we don't believe at the core of our being that we are "the beloved of God," then we are most susceptible to the devil's wiles, which can cause us to fall away from God and destroy us as leaders.

Therefore our identity, our sense of value and worth, is where Satan will most likely launch his attack. Jesus entered the wilderness

"IT DOES NOT MATTER HOW SMALL THE SINS ARE, PROVIDED THAT THEIR CUMULATIVE EFFECT IS TO EDGE THE PERSON AWAY FROM THE LIGHT AND OUT INTO THE NOTHING. . . . INDEED, THE SAFEST ROAD TO HELL IS THE GRADUAL ONE—THE GENTLE SLOPE, SOFT UNDERFOOT, WITHOUT SUDDEN TURNINGS, WITHOUT MILESTONES, WITHOUT SIGNPOSTS."

C. S. Lewis, *The Screwtape Letters*

with his identity secure. He knew his value because of the place he had in the Father's heart. So it starts here for us too. If we are not deeply sure of the place we have in our Father's heart, we are likely to experience *role diversion* or *role confusion.*

ROLE DIVERSION

If our sense of worth does not come from above, we will seek it through the approval of others. Sadly, Christian leaders often are people-pleasers rather than God-pleasers. We allow people's expectations to define us and their affirmations or displeasures to control us. This can be demonstrated when pastoral leaders are diverted from their primary call "to prepare God's people for works of service" (Ephesians 4:12). God's people are to do the work of ministry, which in turn builds up the body of Christ. What happens when a pastor doesn't equip the saints but does the work alone? One major role diversion for a pastor is becoming the *primary caregiver.* In many church traditions the role of caregiver has been professionalized, making hospital visitation, grief ministry and counseling central to the pastor's portfolio. Yet the New Testament clearly states that the church *members* are to care for one another. When pastors are asked why they aren't preparing God's people for ministry, the answer often is, "I am expected to be present when life turns difficult. If I fail at providing care, I have failed as a pastor."

Early in the church's history the apostles refused to succumb to a similar temptation. A dispute about food distribution arose between some Greek-speaking and Hebrew-speaking widows of the church. The dispute was brought to the apostles. They could have become directly involved, which would have changed their God-given ministry. Yet they wisely avoided this diversion, saying, "It would not be right for us to neglect the ministry of the word of God in order to wait on tables" (Acts 6:2). Doing good can become the enemy of the best.

ROLE CONFUSION

So, if we are not grounded in the truth that in Christ we are the Father's beloved child, we can easily fall into role diversion. On the other hand, given the shifting sands of cultural change, leaders are also quite susceptible to role confusion.

Scholars note that we are in the midst of a massive church-paradigm transition. Roughly, from the reign of Emperor Constantine, in the early fourth century, to the twentieth century, the church held a favored position in the West. This was the era of Christendom—the reign of Christianity in the Western world.

The role of professional ministry in Christendom was quite static and predictable. Pastors and parishioners alike agreed what Christian leaders should do. The expectations of pastors can be summarized as follows:

- *Teachers of theological tradition.* Pastors learned the doctrine of their particular theological heritage and taught it to people loyal to that same heritage.

- *Caregivers.* Pastors responded to crises in people's lives through hospital visitation, grief ministry and counseling. They were people's rock in time of need.

- *Symbols of the sacred.* The clergy were the public face of the holy and sacred institutions of the church. The clergy were highly respected because of the sacred role they played.

- *Presiders over rites of passage.* Pastors were the principle figures at the marker moments of people's lives: baptism, confirmation, marriage and death.

Clear, mutual expectations led to a relatively low levels of stress and anxiety.

The collapse of this paradigm—Christendom is no more—is the challenge Christian leaders face today. The friendly and supportive cultural environment in which ministry is done is largely gone. The church is struggling with what it means to be a missional body, as it was in the first three centuries of its existence. A different kind of leader is needed today. Yet many long for the church of the past and want their pastors to act as if Christendom still exists. Others, fearing the demise of the church if it does not become missional again, are demanding a different kind of leader. Sometimes, pastors feel as if they are taffy in a taffy pull.

Should a leader be a prophet, teacher, resource person, enabler, religious expert, preacher, counselor, therapist, CEO, facilitator, leader, equipper, administrator, shepherd, social activist—or all of the above? When you put together the composite expectations, it is an impossible situation.

Heeding the multiple voices of expectations can lead to a life without clear boundaries—role confusion. One pastor expressed this role confusion well: "I felt guilty every time I made a call or headed to the office. 'I should be at home right now,' I reckoned. 'What kind of husband and father am I?' Sitting at home I found myself thinking, 'I should be out making calls tonight. What kind of pastor am I?' "[2]

We have two choices: either define our agenda based on our value and calling from God or be defined by others. Unless we clearly know who we are and what God has called us to do, and thereby define our expectations biblically, people will impose their own expectations on us.

This challenging context of ministry is only the prelude to a more specific assault by Satan. In military strategy terms, Satan is preparing the battlefield through an air assault, which will be followed by the ground attack. We are the battlefield on which this war is fought.

THE MAJOR TEMPTATIONS LEADERS FACE

Jesus entered the wilderness armed for battle: he clearly knew (1) who he was to his Father, and (2) the mission he was called to do. Though Jesus served people, he first lived under the pleasure of and in obedience to his Father. With his identity secure, he could address the particular stratagems of Satan. How about you? If you do not keep returning to your identity in the heart of the Father, then you are liable to be shot down by Satan. Satan will use the classic triad to tempt you: money, power and sex.

Money. After forty days of fasting, Satan begins with the obvious. Jesus is naturally famished, so Satan uses this to challenge Jesus' identity: "If you are the Son of God, tell these stones to become bread" (Matthew 4:3). Satan reduces life to the material. Satisfy your needs. This is the temptation of comfortable, Western society. Place your security in what you accumulate.

For Christian leaders the temptation is to adopt a comfortable lifestyle and live at ease. In the *Screwtape Letters,* C. S. Lewis examines temptation from Satan's perspective. The devil Uncle Wormwood is schooling his nephew Screwtape in ways to neutralize the faith of a new follower of Christ. Wormwood says: "Prosperity knits a man to the World. He feels that he is 'finding his place in it,' while really it is finding its place in him. His increasing reputation, his widening circles of acquaintances, his sense of importance, the growing pressure of absorbing and agreeable work, build in him a sense of being at home on Earth, which is just what we want."[3] If the desire to preserve our own comfortable lifestyle becomes dominant, we will be afraid to challenge the idolatry of greed or offend those who donate to our ministry.

Jesus counters Satan by quoting Scripture, "It is written: 'Man does not live on bread alone, but on every word that comes from the mouth of God'" (Matthew 4:4). In other words, build your life on the eternal perspective of spiritual wisdom, not merely on the material and tangible, as if they are all there is.

Power. The next two temptations Jesus faces have to do with different aspects of power. The devil dangles the temptation of the spectacular before Jesus. Do something dramatic to show that you are in fact the Son of God. Remove the veil that wraps your deity in human flesh.

> Then the devil took him to the holy city and had him stand on the highest point of the temple. "If you are the Son of God," he said, "throw yourself down. For it is written:
>
> "'He will command his angels
>   concerning you,'
> and they will lift you up in their
>   hands,

so that you will not strike your foot against a stone.' " (Matthew 4:5-6)

Even the devil can quote Scripture.

Satan is saying, "Forget servanthood, Jesus, put your power on display. Show us your deity." What an appeal to ego! How subtly success and personal kingdom-building can attack one's spirit. "Oh to be the star of whom all speak well." If we are not secure in our identity as the beloved of the Father, we will seek to fill this deficit with the praise of people. Our value will be determined by the size of our ministry and our relative position in the organizational chart. We will judge ourselves as a success or failure by comparing ourselves to the achievements of others.

Then Satan leads Jesus to a high mountain and shows him the kingdoms of this world and their splendor, "'All this I will give you,' he said, 'if you will bow down and worship me'" (Matthew 4:9). In other words, "Go for the glory, forget the cross. Abandon servanthood, and grasp the prize."

Leaders with a vision of what can be are often tempted to allow the vision to become an ideal (a god). Achieving the vision is so important to the worth of the leader that people become mere tools to fulfill his or her ego. To the leader with such an inflated self-importance, any opposition to the vision is considered a threat, the voice of the enemy. When a person dares to raise a question regarding God's "anointed," he or she faces spiritual abuse, often being defamed as opponents with a critical spirit.

Jesus recognized these temptations to grab power as ultimately an attack on God himself. Jesus was being asked to usurp the place of his Father, who he came to serve. In defense, Jesus constantly reminded himself of his place in the Father's heart and his call to carry out the work of redemption.

Sex. Sexual addictions through pornography or extramarital affairs are at an epidemic level. Rarely does a week go by that we don't hear of some high-profile leader taken down through the breaking of this covenantal trust.

Though Christian leaders may be enticed to succumb to sexual temptations in order to relieve the stresses of leadership or to fulfill a fantasy of desirability, it can never be excused. It is broadly recognized that when leaders inappropriately cross relational boundaries, this is fundamentally an abuse of power and position. Whether it is a male or female leader, connections made initially in the context of spiritual nurture and comfort can turn from healthy affection and appreciation to a powerful sensual draw. Leaders cannot be too careful to guard their own hearts and hold strict guidelines about when and where appointments with the opposite sex are kept.

With the advent of the Internet, we now have the technology to "cleave sexual desire from personal relationship."[4] The siren song of lust beckons us, "For the moment I will make you happy. Escape into the fantasy world of airbrushed images. You can possess this lovely object of desire." John Piper writes, "The power of temptation is the prospect that it will make me happier."[5]

> "THE FATHER OF LIES CROONS AND WOOS LIKE A TRAVELING PEDDLER, PROMISING THE MOON AND DELIVERING DISASTER."
>
> Max Lucado, *No Wonder They Call Him the Savior*

It must be acknowledged that each of these sins can have deep and entangled roots within our spirit. Since they are the primary ways that Satan will want to discredit our leadership, we will likely need the assistance of a skilled Christian counselor, spiritual friend and/or spiritual director to help us look courageously deep within. All we can do in this lesson is identify the key potential pitfalls and the core issues at the base of all sin.

FIGHTING TEMPTATION

So whether it is the allure of comfort (money), power or sex, we fight all these idols by realizing that each of them promises satisfaction, but they can only deliver momentary pleasure. They are cotton candy to the soul. All of these temptations dangled before Christian leaders by the evil one are attempts to get us to believe that our primary contentment and ultimate identity are found somewhere besides being beloved sons and daughters of God. Jesus resisted severing the relationship with his Father by quoting Scripture about his identity in his Father. John Piper writes, "When my thirst for joy and meaning and passion are satisfied by the presence and power of Christ, the power of sin is broken. We do not yield to the offer of sandwich meat when we can smell the steak sizzling on the grill."[6]

---

[1]J. I. Packer, *Knowing God* (Downers Grove, Ill.: InterVarsity Press, 1973), p. 181.

[2]Glenn McDonald, "Imagining a New Church," *Christian Century,* September 8-15, 1999, p. 850.

[3]C. S. Lewis, *The Screwtape Letters* (New York: Macmillan, 1961), p. 132.

[4]Philip Yancey, *Rumors of Another World* (Grand Rapids: Zondervan, 2003), p. 84.

[5]John Piper, *Future Grace* (Sisters, Ore.: Multnomah, 1995), p. 334.

[6]Ibid., p. 335.

Leadership Exercise: Naming Our Temptations

The first step in defeating temptation is to recognize our particular susceptibilities to the schemes of the devil. When we name the ways that we are particularly vulnerable to the evil one, we are well on our way to mounting a defense.

SHORING UP THE FOUNDATION

The authors make the fundamental point that the battle must be fought on the secure foundation of our identity in Christ. Just as Jesus faced down the devil in the wilderness secure in the knowledge that he was the beloved Son of the Father, we too must be rooted in the truth that we are the beloved adopted sons and daughters of God. Restate in your own words why this is a necessary basis from which to start, and why we are most susceptible to temptation if this reality is not in place.

THE ATMOSPHERE OF LEADERSHIP (AIR ASSAULT)

We live in a changing cultural environment that serves as the atmosphere in which we minister today. This changing environment can lead to role diversion and role confusion.

Role diversion. In your leadership role, what are the expectations that can divert you from what you expect of yourself?

How does the way the apostles in Acts 6:1-4 handled their temptation to role diversion serve as a model for the way you might handle the similar temptations today?

Role confusion. Because of the changing context of ministry today, how does this affect expectations of the role you are to play?

Role expectations are often a composite of the expectations of the people we serve. Check all that apply to you:

____ prophet	____ counselor	____ administrator
____ teacher	____ therapist	____ shepherd
____ resource person	____ CEO	____ social activist
____ enabler	____ facilitator	____ other_____
____ religious expert	____ leader	
____ preacher	____ equipper	

The authors said, "We have two choices: either define our agenda based on our value and calling from God or be defined by others." How would you define your leadership role so that you can set expectations for others?

THE SPECIFIC TEMPTATIONS OF A LEADER (GROUND ATTACK)

Satan has used predictable means to get at leaders: money, power and sex.

Money: The lure of material comfort. The longing to live a comfortable life can cause leaders to lose their leadership edge. How might this be true of you?

Power: The lure of ego. The longing to be known and exalted can cause leaders to place themselves at the center. How might this be true of you?

Sex: The lure of self-gratification. The longing for instant gratification to relieve stress can cause leaders to use others to make themselves feel good. How might this be true of you?

THE SCHEMES OF THE EVIL ONE

Each of us has susceptibilities to the way Satan can bring us down. What have you noticed about where you might be most vulnerable?

CONCLUSION

A Chinese proverb says that "the beginning of wisdom is to call things by their right name." There is power and freedom in naming the issues that we face. This is the first and most important step in defeating temptation.

Going Deeper

Foster, Richard. *Money, Sex and Power.* London: Hodder & Stoughton, 1999.

Lewis, C. S. *The Screwtape Letters.* New York: Macmillan, 1961.

11 / Conquering Criticism

Looking Ahead

Memory Verse: Psalm 139:23-24
Bible Study: Matthew 18:15-35
Reading: Barriers Become Bridges
Leadership Exercise: Reconsidering Resistance

 Core Truth

How do Christian leaders respond to the opposition they frequently face?

Leading disciples understand that their character and capacities are both revealed and refined by how they respond to the criticism, conflict, and other forms of resistance they encounter. They discipline themselves to view these antagonisms as potential allies in their quest for more Christ-like maturity, wisdom and influence.

1. Identify key words or phrases in the question and answer above, and state their meaning in your own words.

2. Restate the core truth in your own words.

3. What questions or issues does the core truth raise for you?

Memory Verse Study Guide

Copy the entire text here:

Memory Verse: Psalm 139:23-24

Psalm 139 is a meditation on the omnipresence and the omniscience of God. These twin realities help to form the basis of a leader's confidence and humility, especially in the face of the resistance he or she meets on the path of leadership.

1. What difference might it make to a leader that God is always with (omnipresence) and that God knows everything about (omniscience) him or her?

2. Few people today get very excited about the notion of being "searched" or "tested." Why does the psalmist want God to do these things to him?

3. The psalmist speaks of his "anxious thoughts." What are some of the anxieties that come with leadership?

4. What are some of the "offensive ways" that sometimes inhabit a leader's life?

5. The psalmist's final prayer is "lead me in the way everlasting." What does this petition and the words that come before it reveal about his ultimate ambition?

Inductive Bible Study Guide

Bible Study: Matthew 18:15-35

Matthew 18 makes it clear that Jesus never envisioned a conflict-free Christian community or a church where issues would not have to be wrestled with strenuously. At the same time, Jesus laid out some clear principles and processes to resolve such matters. In this chapter we are focusing on the specific issue of *how a leader handles criticism of and conflict in his or her leadership.* Matthew 18 offers some crucial perspectives that help guide leaders in their resolution work.

1. *Read Matthew 18:15-17.* Here Jesus lays out a pattern of due process for resolving grievances. List the four steps he lays out and the values you think are being communicated.

   Step   **Values**

   1.

   2.

   3.

   4.

2. Do some research on verses 18-20. Verse 19 is often taken as a promise that Jesus is present where two or three are gathered in prayer. Given the context of discipline, what other interpretation seems to fit?

3. Read verse 21. What do you think Peter is trying to figure out? Have you ever wrestled with this question yourself?

4. Read verses 22-34. What value is Jesus stressing on how we deal with other people's "debts" (or "trespasses")?

5. How are you comforted, challenged or confused by what Jesus says in verse 35?

6. How has this passage spoken to you?

Reading: Barriers Become Bridges

"He came to that which was his own, but his own did not receive him" (John 1:11). "'No servant is greater than his master.' If they persecuted me, they will persecute you also" (John 15:20).

Sooner or later every leader encounters resistance to his or her leadership. If our Great Leader, Jesus, met it, we can certainly count on experiencing resistance too. It may arise within the leadership team, as it did for Jesus when Judas betrayed him. It may appear among those we are serving, as it did for Christ on Good Friday. Resistance may spring up among powerful interests in our environment; Jesus faced the opposition of the religious and political leaders of his day. It may even come from within our own home. The point is that resistance is not a *possible* part of a leader's life. It is a *certainty*.

> "OFTEN THE CROWD DOES NOT RECOGNIZE A LEADER UNTIL HE HAS GONE, AND THEN THEY BUILD A MONUMENT FOR HIM WITH THE STONES THEY THREW AT HIM IN LIFE."
>
> J. Oswald Sanders, *Spiritual Leadership*

THE FACES OF RESISTANCE

Passive. Sometimes, this resistance is subtle. People often express mild discomfort or disagreement with their leader's personality or actions. They may pull back from involvement or simply not show up. They whisper and grumble behind the leader's back. They speak behind closed doors about how the effort could be led better. Perhaps they are passive-aggressive. They express their frustrations at a level that isn't blatantly contentious but nonetheless gets attention.

Assertive. Sometimes the resistance is more overt. People express direct and even heated concern about a leader's character, competency or course of action. They may write critical letters or ask for a meeting where they can vent their grievances or worries. They talk often and openly with others about their concerns. They may gather a group to mount organized opposition to what is being planned or advanced. They are set on redirecting or stopping the leader before further "damage" is done.

Aggressive. There are times when resistance is simply toxic. People may send anonymous, flaming letters to the leadership or other people of influence. They may circulate public denouncements, maligning the leader's motivations or actions. They search for and interpret all relevant data as further evidence of the leader's bad character or dark intentions. They stir up suspicion, anger or fear in as many people as they can. They are bent on destroying the leader or the leader's credibility or cause.

THE DANGEROUS EFFECTS OF RESISTANCE

Given these realities, it is safe to say that unless leading disciples find creative ways of responding to resistance, it will have one or more very damaging effects on their life and influence.

Active denial. Desiring to focus on the mission without distraction, leaders under fire may deny that significant resistance exists or that it should be taken seriously. Often these leaders surround themselves with people who validate the present course of action, leaving others in despair of being heard. These leaders may have enough support that the number of people who walk away frustrated or hurt don't make much of a dent. On the other hand, such leaders may be puzzled as to why their mission isn't succeeding or are shocked when a large group comes demanding their head.

Involuntary shutdown. The consistent pressure of unresolved resistance can also cause leaders to simply shut down emotionally. Unable to deny the serious static in the system but also unable to cope with it, these leaders turn off the radio. They increasingly fail to listen to the complaints or concerns of others because it is simply too hard to live with them. These leaders appear somewhat glazed and dazed, and others wonder why they don't "get it."

Overcompensation. Some leaders handle resistance by obsessing over their critics. As Keith Miller said in conversation once, they allow others "rent-free space in their mind." They expend excessive resources trying to please and pacify every critic, as if this were possible. Or they may go on a defensive rampage, desperately trying to refute all critics or prove themselves right in character or action. They end up looking terribly insecure, further undermining their leadership credibility and becoming diverted from their creative mission.

> "I HAVE NO AMBITION TO GOVERN MEN. IT IS A PAINFUL AND THANKLESS OFFICE."
>
> Thomas Jefferson, *The Writings of Thomas Jefferson*

Lash back. Other leaders simply respond to resistance in kind. They become highly critical of others, particularly those they suspect or know to be opposing their leadership. They may exhibit behavior that appears dictatorial or out of control. They rage at their actual or perceived opponents in a way that wounds many and makes others lose confidence in them.

Burnout. Ultimately, resistance that is not addressed creatively can frazzle leaders' nerves and overly burden their hearts. Prolonged contact with conflict and criticism wears them down. It robs them of the joy of ministry or leadership. Eventually, many once-enthusiastic leaders simply want "out."

THE SOURCES OF RESISTANCE

Clearly it is important for Christian leaders to creatively respond to resistance in order to eliminate its dangerous effects. Recognizing the possible *sources* of resistance is key. In this respect, the Bible gives us some very helpful clues.

Sin causes resistance. In Galatians, the apostle Paul suggests that if we all lived with a consistently vital connection to God, then our interactions with one another would exhibit "love, joy, peace, patience, kindness, goodness, faithfulness, gentleness and self-control" (Galatians 5:22-25), which would make us wonderful partners in pursuit of the good. The reality, of course, is that none enjoy this unbroken communion. We are infected with pride and insecurity (a "sinful nature") that gives birth to "hatred, discord, jealousy, fits of rage, selfish ambition, dissensions, factions and envy" (Galatians 5:20-21). These bad fruits affect our relationships and impede the progress of good in this world.

Spiritual forces cause resistance. Paul also reminds us that our struggle is not only "against flesh and blood, but . . . against the powers of this dark world and against the spiritual forces of evil in the heavenly realms" (Ephesians 6:12). Maybe you've been in a situation where no amount of organizational sweat or savvy seems able to overcome the resistance you face for the simple reason that you are meeting opposition at the supernatural level—"powers" and "forces" that don't want to see the purposes of the King or kingdom prevail. Christians know that on the cross Christ struck the decisive blow to such powers. The powers' days are numbered. But they continue to resist, and we still skirmish with them.

Psychosocial causes. There are tremendous psychological and social differences between people. Paul celebrates this fact when he says: "Now the body is not made up of one part but of many. . . . If the whole body were an eye, where would the sense of hearing be? If the whole body were an ear, where would the sense of smell be? But in fact God has arranged the parts in the body, every one of them, just as he wanted them to be" (1 Corinthians 12:14, 17-18). Later, in 2 Corinthians 10—11, however, Paul has been beaten by this body, stammering to defend his leadership against the criticism of various members of the body. The splendid diversity of God's creatures has two challeng-

> "LEADERS MUST MAKE ROOM FOR THE POSSIBILITY AND AFFIRM THE VALUE OF A 'LOYAL OPPOSITION' WHO RAISE AWKWARD QUESTIONS AND PROVIDE POSITIVE CRITIQUE."
>
> Eddie Gibbs, *LeadershipNext*

ing implications for Christian leaders.

First, people respond to *change* differently. As we saw in chapter eight, only about 16 percent of the people we meet are "innovators" or "early adopters." When presented with a novel idea, they'll try it. Thirty-four percent are what we might call "middle adopters." They want to see the benefits before jumping on board. Another 34 percent are "late adopters." They are skeptics who need lots of evidence and time to be convinced of the worth of an innovation. The final 16 percent are the "maybe never adopters." They likely will never feel peaceful about change. In the church environment, they may walk away mad or sad, or remain as irritants. These varying responses challenge a leader to be both respectful of people and patient about the length of time it may take to build support for a cause.

Second, people respond to *communication* differently. A significant part of leadership is helping people to catch and pursue a vision. But not everyone responds to our communication efforts in the same way. The Bible suggests that sometimes this is because some individuals do not "have ears to hear" (Ezekiel 12:2; Luke 8:8). They may not want to disturb their familiar or comfortable arrangements. They may have a vested interest in keeping things as they are. Or they may be too busy or distracted to listen to the leader's case, much less the call of God. In many instances, however, the resistance to leadership is less an issue of personal openness than how the message is presented.

Some years ago Harvard University's Howard Gardner popularized an approach to education that has come to be known as "Multiple Intelligence Theory." The theory suggests that in order for influencers to truly and fully communicate with people in a life-penetrating, personally motivating way, they must recognize that not all people learn in the same manner. Gardner identifies seven different learning styles. Take a look at "Leveraging Learning Styles" (pp. 159-60) and think about what this means for leading people in your setting.

At least some of the resistance Christian leaders face is due to the fact that we have not adequately respected or responded to the diverse ways that people adapt to change. It is, of course, possible that we are simply dealing with sin-blinded or devil-driven people. Before making this assumption, however, good leaders discipline themselves to ask if *they* might change something in order to produce better results.

> "CONFRONTING ANOTHER PERSON WITH THE TRUTH IS ONE OF THE GREATEST RISKS OF LOVE WE WILL EVER TAKE."
>
> M. Scott Peck, *The Road Less Traveled*

CREATIVE RESPONSES TO RESISTANCE

Finally, resistance is a dimension of relationship, and relationship—as Jesus models for us—is the ground of all leadership. How we work with this ground both *reveals* and *refines* our character and capacities. It displays what we are *made of* and if we are *willing to be made* more than we already are. When we respond to resistance with immaturity or ignorance, we enhance resistance, which becomes a barrier to further effective leadership. When we respond wisely, those who resist can actually strengthen us by demanding something better

of us and thereby increasing the respect and buy-in of others. What might have been a barrier becomes a bridge.

Jesus, the great bridge-builder, has much to teach us about this dimension of leadership. He himself faced so much resistance yet handled it in a way that actually increased his stature and influence. Here are some practical principles from his life.

Lean on your Father in prayer. On the night of his arrest, Jesus was facing tremendous resistance. He was being attacked by sinful human beings and spiritual powers alike. He was even being betrayed and abandoned by those he loved. Jesus was struggling with the desire to comfort his own flesh by escaping the coming pain. Later he was ridiculed, beaten, tortured and crucified. In the garden of Gethsemane—which literally means "the olive press"—Jesus was the olive being crushed. And what seeped out of him was a prayer to his Father: "d'*Abba,* Father,' he said, 'everything is possible for you. Take this cup from me. Yet not what I will, but what you will'" (Mark 14:35-36).

The resilience and potency of Christ's leadership is impossible to explain apart from his intimate communion with his Father. Jesus named his Father as the source of his *love* (John 15:9-10), the font of his *wisdom* (John 15:15) and the supply of his *power* (Matthew 26:53). Jesus lived continually in his Father's presence. Thus it comes as no surprise that Jesus sought his Father's grace when he faced the greatest resistance. And God granted him the strength to do God's will.

What about you? If you do not have a greater strength to lean on, if you do not have an unflagging supporter to steady you, if you do not have someone to whom you can go to remind you that you are beloved no matter what others are saying about or doing to you, you will be crushed. But if you have the unfailing Father, you have an identity and security that can stand any pressure. You can pray, "Give me the strength I need, Father, to respond to this time, to fulfill your will," and God will supply it.

Let your furnace become a crucible. During challenging times God sometimes strengthens us not by patting us on the back and encouraging us to keep doing what we are doing, but by calling us to endure hardship with patience. The reality is that Jesus is the *only* person who did not make profound mistakes while ministering to others. All other leaders achieve greatness only as they *learn* while ministering. That is why Christian leaders sooner or later develop the discipline of self-examination. Because they know that even something as cruel as a cross can actually be the crucible of redemption, they also know that sometimes criticism or opposition can be the touch of the loving hand of God seeking to shape a better future.

We remember King David as a great leader because—in spite of his famous errors—he learned to say:

> Search me, O God, and know my heart;
>   test me and know my anxious
>   thoughts.
> See if there is any offensive way in me,
>   and lead me in the way everlasting.
>   (Psalm 139:23-24)

When under attack, it's always tempting to look for the faults of *others*. But perhaps God is using the resistance of others to shed light on *us*. An absolutely essential discipline we leaders need to learn is asking the brutally honest questions about our character, our competence or our course of action. Here are a few examples.

- Character questions. Is there anything about my personal motivations or conduct that is undermining people's ability to trust me or give themselves to our cause? Have I any sin (pride, anger, greed, lust, gluttony, envy, deceit, or sloth) that others are aware of and I have been denying? David had Nathan to help him see the truth (2 Samuel 12:1-13); who could help me?

- Competency questions. Are there legitimate performance problems or value issues that my critics are spotting? Am I working beyond my skills, abilities and gifts more than I've recognized up to this point? Is more training or team-building needed? Is it time to bring in the complementary gifts of others? Who are the mature leaders who could help me get some less emotionally charged perspective on possible gaps?

- Course of action questions. Is there some course correction needed here? Do we need to take another look at our vision, goals or timeline? Have I been too impatient in view of the way people adapt to changes? Have I done enough listening? Is there some part of my planning or preparation that now needs redefinition? Am I communicating our vision in the variety of ways needed to help a broad range of people understand the value of what we're seeking to be and do?

When was the last time you thanked a

critic for being the window through which God's light moved more deeply into your life? With God's help, the painful furnace of resistance can become the creative crucible that refines your leadership and strengthens your ministry.

Refuse to be undone by untruths. As we underlined in chapter three, humility is a major mark of biblical leadership. At the same time, there are situations when the needed response is not repentance but *resilience*. It's simply untrue that where smoke is billowing around a leader, the fire of leadership failure *must be* behind it. Consider all the accusatory billows that surrounded the ministry of Jesus. Yet we know that he was not a poor leader. We live in a world where the fastest liar often wins in the popular imagination. The more colorful the lie, the more it seems to fit some melodramatic story line, the more ready people are to believe it.

Christian leaders cannot exhaust their energies obsessively defending themselves against untruth. Think how little energy Jesus expended trying to explain himself to the likes of Herod or Pilate. Abraham Lincoln once answered a scalding letter from a voter by saying: "Madam, if I spent all my time responding to accusations like you have made, I would have no time left to serve your country." How about you? Could it be time to stop trying to disprove an untruth by more talking, and trust that the truth will come out by more walking?

Eliminate enemies. One of the cruelest political opponents Lincoln ever faced was a man named Edwin Stanton. Stanton not only assailed Lincoln's viewpoints, he publicly ridiculed his physical appearance. Later, when Lincoln had ascended to the presidency, he nominated none other than Edwin Stanton to serve in the hugely important post of Secretary of War. Lincoln's advisers protested, "Don't you understand that this man is your *enemy,* Mr. President?" Lincoln's response was classic: "Do I not destroy my enemies when I make them my *friends?*" Stanton went on to be a simply brilliant cabinet member, and at the president's funeral he delivered one of Lincoln's most devoted eulogies.

There are, of course, some opponents who are simply so unreasonable, so angry or so philosophically different that it would be dangerous or disastrous to bring them into the circle. It is challenging, however, to note that Paul, the greatest apostle, actually started out as one of its most bloodthirsty critics. What if Jesus had never bothered to teach Paul that "love is patient [and] kind" (1 Corinthians 13:4)? Is it so unthinkable that some of the critics you face might actually help advance God's cause if you could only find a way to make them friends?

Extend muscular grace. Jesus was neither a pushover nor naive about people. Jesus addressed wrongdoing very assertively. He issued searing critiques of the Pharisees' self-righteousness. He overturned the tables of the moneychangers, who were desecrating the temple and ripping off the poor. In scores of ways, Jesus actively championed God's concerns and defended the weak. But it's also striking that when Jesus was *personally* attacked, he didn't repay evil for evil. In a su-

> "ENDURANCE IS NOT JUST THE ABILITY TO BEAR A HARD THING, BUT TO TURN IT INTO GLORY."
>
> William Barclay, Daily Study Bible series

preme revelation of his character, Jesus prayed from the cross for those who crucified him and rejoiced in his agony: "Father, forgive them, for they do not know what they are doing" (Luke 23:34).

If you are called to be a Christian leader, then you are called to serve where some will not always understand what you are doing or how their attitudes and actions affect you. You will not always be able to win them over, no matter how hard you try, and they may not stop trying to defeat you. There are times when, as leaders, our only succor is the knowledge that we are in excellent company. Jesus hung in that place personally. He didn't just *say,* "Do good to those who hate you, bless those who curse you, pray for those who mistreat you" (Luke 6:27-28). Jesus *lived* it with courage upon a cross. He showed us what gracious forbearance under the most extreme resistance looks like. We can certainly be "leaders" of a sort without this kind of courageous, muscular grace. But we will not be *Christian* leaders.

Build amid the bombing. It's amazing, isn't it, how even in his dying Jesus never stopped leading people into a better vision of living? With his last breaths, Jesus formed a new family (John 19:26-27) and ushered a repentant thief into paradise (Luke 23:39-43). There's a lesson here. Even under destructive pressure, leaders keep doing constructive things. During the worst of the famous blitzkrieg that leveled most of London during World War II, Winston Churchill remained in the city. The prime minister sat in a basement as the bombing reduced much of the splendid city to rubble. Churchill wasn't bemoaning his poor fortune but planning the D-Day invasion and the reconstruction of Europe.

There will always be "bombers" of one kind or another. But as Teddy Roosevelt once observed:

> It is not the critic who counts: not the man who points out how the strong man stumbles or where the doer of deeds could have done better. The credit belongs to the man who is actually in the arena, whose face is marred by dust and sweat and blood, who strives valiantly, who errs and comes up short again and again, because there is no effort without error or shortcomings but who knows the great . . . devotions, who spends himself for a worthy cause; who, at the best, knows, in the end, the triumph of high achievement, and who, at the worst, if he fails, at least he fails while daring greatly, so that his place shall never be with those cold and timid souls who know neither victory nor defeat.[1]

Jesus put it more succinctly: "In this world you will have trouble. But take heart! I have overcome the world" (John 16:33). Dare to trust this: What may look to us at the beginning like the bane or barrier of resistance can become instead a bridge to a maturity, wisdom and influence more like Jesus Christ's.

SUPPLEMENTAL RESOURCE: LEVERAGING LEARNING STYLES

Verbal/Linguistic Learners

These people respond well to the written and spoken word. Tell them the story. Clarify the needs and benefits. Invite them to imagine themselves in the story. Ask them to distill the cause to a "bottom line," and if the story is a good one, they tend to take on the message and mission.

Interpersonal Learners

These people don't learn well through proclaimed truth—no matter how articulate. Their learning is enhanced through a personal touch. They imagine and integrate life in terms of relationships. Invite them into the group where the mission is being discovered and lived out. God communicates with them through the community.

Bodily/Kinesthetic Learners
These people best connect to an idea when they are actively doing something. Don't tell them; take them. Immerse them in the environment where the needs are tangible and the opportunities can be tasted. Give them a practical job in the cause. Then they will truly see what the leader has in mind.

Intrapersonal Learners
These people need time to discern their inner response to change. Respect their need to get their inner world in order before jumping in. Invite them to share the variety of thoughts and feelings that they are having. Honor their desire to act with forethought and integrity. Rush them, and you'll be rejected.

Logical/Mathematical Learners
These people want to know the facts before taking on the acts. They want to see the pattern, order and logical structure of things. Give them the details. Invite them to research the subject and come to their own conclusions about the needs or the value of the approach being suggested. These thinkers can become great partners.

Musical/Rhythmic Learners
These people take in information best when it is presented in musical or rhythmic form. Provide them with songs that express the heart and mind of what you're leading. Come up with cheers or chants that do the same or encourage them to devise these choruses for your mission.

Visual/Spatial Learners
These people use their eyes and imagination to study a cause. Provide them with colorful pictures of the possible. Describe in visual terms the impact of the work you're advocating. Welcome them to help you frame the mission in visible form, and the picture will become theirs in a very personal and motivating way.

(This material is also relevant to "Helping Others See" [chap. 9].)

[1]Theodore Roosevelt, "Citizenship in a Republic," a speech given at the Sorbonne, Paris, April 23, 1910. See <www.theodoreroosevelt .org/life/quotes.htm>.

Leadership Exercise: Reconsidering Resistance

1. Where have you seen any of the "Faces of Resistance" (p. 153) in your past or present leadership experience?

    _____ passive

    _____ active

    _____ aggressive

2. Which of the "Dangerous Effects" (pp. 153-54) can you relate to?

    _____ active denial   _____ involuntary shutdown

    _____ overcompensation   _____ lash back

    _____ burnout

    What other effects of prolonged resistance have you seen or experienced?

3. As you think about your own leadership experience of dealing with criticism, conflict or opposition, what role would you assign to the following sources of resistance?

    Sin

    Spiritual forces

4. When it comes to adaptability to change, where do you see yourself on the following scale?

    |——|

    Early Adopter   Middle Adopter   Later Adopter   Rarely Adopter
    "I'm in!"   "Show me"   "Really prove it"   "It's just fine now"

How do you think this influences the way you lead?

5. When it comes to receptivity to communication, which of the learning styles (pp. 159-60) best describes you?

____ verbal/linguistic learner   ____ logical/mathematical learner
____ interpersonal learner   ____ musical/rhythmic learner
____ bodily/kinesthetic learner   ____ visual/spatial learner
____ intrapersonal learner

What might be done to capture the imagination and heart of some of the people who have a learning style different from yours?

6. Which of the following creative responses to resistance strike you as particularly important or particularly difficult?

____ lean on your Father in prayer   ____ refuse to be undone by untruth
____ let your furnace become a crucible   ____ extend muscular grace
____ eliminate enemies by making them friends   ____ build amid the bombing

What are some other responses or approaches you believe are important?

7. Which of all of the possible responses (see question 6) will you intentionally focus on as you meet criticism, conflict or other opposition in days ahead?

Going Deeper

Backus, William. *Telling Each Other the Truth*. Minneapolis: Bethany House, 1985.

Gardner, Howard. *Frames of Mind: The Theory of Multiple Intelligences*. New York: Basic Books, 1983.

Hauck, Kenneth. *Antagonists in the Church*. Minneapolis: Augsburg, 1988.

McNeal, Reggie. *A Work of Heart: How God Shapes Spiritual Leaders*. San Francisco: Jossey Bass, 2000.

Shelley, Marshall. *Well-Intentioned Dragons*. Waco, Tex.: Word Books, 1985.

12 / Defeating Discouragement

LOOKING AHEAD

Memory Verse: Galatians 6:9
Bible Study: 2 Timothy 4:9-18
Reading: Those Who Rise
Leadership Exercise: Stepping Up, Out and On Your Way

 Core Truth

How do Christian leaders avoid being buried by the weight of discouragement?

Leading disciples know that whether they finish the journey of leadership well depends greatly on how effectively they cope with the crushing emotions that can beset them in the effort to do good. They are careful to take the deliberate and repeated steps required to keep rising above these painful pressures so that they may complete their mission.

1. Identify key words or phrases in the question and answer above, and state their meaning in your own words.

2. Restate the core truth in your own words.

3. What questions or issues does the core truth raise for you?

Memory Verse Study Guide

Copy the entire text here:

Memory Verse: Galatians 6:9

Few leaders can claim the variety of disheartening circumstances the apostle Paul faced over the course of his life (see for example 2 Corinthians 11:23-28). In this Bible study we'll see that Paul did experience moments of pain and questioning. Yet in our memory verse from Paul's letter to the disciples at Galatia, he pounds out the heartbeat of a hope and passion that is much more representative of his life.

1. What do you think Paul means by "doing good" (v. 9)? Reading the verses that precede this one may be helpful in understanding the context.

2. What does the apostle suggest is the possible negative result that may come from the prolonged effort to do good?

3. What does Paul say will occur if we can avoid letting this happen?

4. What do you suppose Paul means by "at the proper time"?

Inductive Bible Study Guide

Bible Study: 2 Timothy 4:9-18

In this passage we meet one of history's greatest leaders at one of his lowest moments. Written in about A.D. 67, the second letter to Timothy is Paul's last communication to his son in the faith. Paul is now in prison in Rome for the final time. In a very short while, he will be beheaded. Here we get not only a window into the darkness that can overtake even the finest leaders, but also a glimpse of the light that keeps him going in the hardest seasons of life.

1. Sometimes, a world of feeling is communicated in a single request. What is the inner reality that Paul seems to be expressing in verse 9?

2. If you had to assign an adjective to describe Paul's mood in verses 10 and 16, what would it be?

   What appears to have occasioned it?

3. What kind of comfort is Paul seeking in verse 13? What does this say about his condition at this point in his life?

4. Paul doesn't wallow in self-pity regarding the harm brought about by "Alexander the metal-worker" (vv. 14-15). How does Paul deal with this harm, and how might this have prevented discouragement?

5. What are some of the "positives" that Paul holds on to or underlines in the following verses?

v. 11:

v. 14:

v. 17:

6. What is the final hope and assurance that Paul clings on to (v. 18)?

7. In summary, what do we learn from Paul about the antidote to discouragement?

8. What questions or issues does this passage raise for you?

"SO, WHAT DO YOU THINK? WITH GOD ON OUR SIDE LIKE THIS, HOW CAN WE LOSE? . . . THE ONE WHO DIED FOR US—WHO WAS RAISED TO LIFE FOR US!— IS IN THE PRESENCE OF GOD AT THIS VERY MOMENT STICKING UP FOR US. DO YOU THINK ANYONE IS GOING TO BE ABLE TO DRIVE A WEDGE BETWEEN US AND CHRIST'S LOVE FOR US? THERE IS NO WAY! NOT TROUBLE, NOT HARD TIMES, NOT HATRED, NOT HUNGER, NOT HOMELESSNESS, NOT BULLYING THREATS, NOT BACKSTABBING, NOT EVEN THE WORST SINS LISTED IN SCRIPTURE."

Romans 8:31, 34-35, *The Message*

👓 Reading: Those Who Rise

The story is told of a farmer's donkey who stumbled into an old, dry well. For hours the animal brayed piteously as the farmer tried to sort out what to do. Finally, the farmer decided that because the animal was old and the pit was dangerous, he could solve two problems at once. The farmer promptly invited his neighbors over to help him fill in the well. As the first shovel loads of dirt pattered down on top of him, the donkey seemed to sense, somehow, what was happening to him. At first, he brayed and cried out in panic and despair. And then, quite strangely, the animal went silent. The farmer looked down the well and stopped in astonishment. As each spade of dirt struck his back, the donkey simply shook it off. He then shifted his feet and stepped up a bit higher on top of the fallen earth. Many hours and shovel loads later, the donkey rose up over the edge of the well and trotted off!

Under pressure, what leader wouldn't want to be as creative as this donkey? Maybe the donkey comparison isn't too flattering, but who of us doesn't pray that when we encounter pitfalls and dirt loads on the path of leadership, we might be able to rise above them?

SIFTING THE DIRT OF DISCOURAGEMENT

Sometime, every leader feels that he or she is at the bottom of the well—and daylight is shrinking fast. It may be a pit into which the leader has been conscious of slowly and gradually descending. Or the descent may have felt more like a sudden plummet. The leader may have dug it him- or herself, or simply stumbled into it. Regardless of the path of entry, when a leader sifts the dirt that is raining down in such times, it often contains some or all of the following elements.

Disappointment. There are moments when, no matter how hard we and others work toward a goal, things simply don't turn out as we had hoped. We don't get through the agenda or to-do list we've charted. The resources we've anticipated don't materialize. We don't get the response or the results we've expected. Because Christian leaders usually are invested in the outcomes in a more intense way than others may be, the disappointment the leaders feel when it doesn't work out is like a much deeper and darker hole.

Frustration. Sometimes the disappointment is compounded by the sense that others have let us down. They don't embrace what seems to us like such an obviously great vision. They fail to pull their weight or keep their promises. They won't move fast enough or perform to the standard expected. They can't seem to rise above their own parochial interests for the sake of the bigger picture. They behave in selfish or unfathomable ways. As Scripture makes clear, a leader can even get profoundly frustrated with God (see Psalm 13, for example).

Failure. Other times, however, it is our own shovel that slams us in the face. We stand like Peter at the third cock crow (Matthew 26:69-75), at least dimly aware of how weak, stupid, arrogant, duplicitous or incompetent we've been. We wish we could run and hide or find somebody else to take the fall for what we've done, but there is no escaping the fact that we dug our own hole. We expected more of ourselves—or should have. We think, *I'm supposed to be a* leader, *but what an absolute* donkey *I am.*

Worthlessness. And then there are periods when a Christian leader may come to feel like he or she is merely a mule to other people. We think to ourselves: *I do a lot of work. I carry a heavy burden. I get attacked by wolves and flies, and everyone takes it for granted. They get all excited about the newest "racehorse" to show up and forget about the back this show's been riding on. Is it too much to ask for somebody to toss an occasional palm branch in my direction, a mild hosanna? I'd certainly go another mile if I knew I was really valued.*

Loneliness. There is a terrible loneliness to moments like these. Truth be told, however, this sense of painful solitude is a not-too-infrequent theme in a leader's life. In his book *LeadershipNext,* Eddie Gibbs observes:

> There is a loneliness that arises from the calling of a leader. It is the loneliness of visionaries who see beyond their contemporaries and whose ideas fly in the face of beliefs that are unquestioningly accepted by those around them. It is the loneliness of having to make decisions that affect the lives of other people. It is the loneliness of the preacher who carries a burden to deliver a word from God that he or she knows will expose disobedience or faltering faith. It is the loneliness that comes when leaders find themselves deserted, not only by their followers but also by their closest friends.[1]

At his lowest ebb, Jesus experienced this in the Garden of Gethsemane (Mark 14:32-42). And Paul expressed this feeling well when he said, "You know that everyone in the province of Asia has deserted me" (2 Timothy 1:15). Even in the crowd, a leader can feel very much alone.

THE SIGNS OF DISCOURAGEMENT

When a leader says, "I feel like I've lost my heart for this enterprise (or this group of people). My confidence and energy isn't what it used to be and what I want it to be. I think I need someone to talk with me about what's going on so I can begin to climb out of this hole and get back on the journey," it is often because the dirt of discouragement has simply become too heavy. However, the reality is that many leaders don't speak so clearly about their sorrow. Like the donkey in the parable, they bray first in other ways.

Anger. Sometimes discouragement shows itself in anger. Disappointment, frustration and other emotions pile up until there is a breaking point. Like King Saul in the Old Testament, some leaders become pathologically angry people—venting their rage in self-destructive patterns, at coworkers or in their messages to the crowd (1 Samuel 18:1-11). Eventually, this unresolved rage eats them and their leadership alive.

Depression. Often the painful feelings of a discouraged leader turn inward instead of being expressed outward. As with the biblical character Jonah, God calls the leader to face the issues squarely. But the leader runs from this "Nineveh," fleeing to harder work, food or substance abuse, an illicit affair, or some other "Tarsus." The pains, passions and losses swallowed, however, may finally become the whale of depression that swallows the depressed leader (Jonah 2). In his book *Dark Clouds, Silver Linings,* Archibald Hart says the signs of depression may include loss of energy, motivation, pleasure or ability to sleep. More and more of life feels meaningless as the leader descends into the dark pit of sadness.[2]

Resignation. Then there are those who deal with the dirt by simply walking away. When the prophet Elijah found his best efforts insufficient to overcome the corruption of Queen Jezebel and the cult of Baal, he resigned his role. "I have had enough, LORD," he said (see 1 Kings 19:1-10). Every year, huge numbers of Christian leaders do just that. Crushed by the dirt of discouragement, they simply lay down their leadership commission. Both authors of this book have been to the bottom of the well and have experienced parts of all of the issues discussed. Maybe you are there yourself right now or know someone who is. Perhaps you will find yourself in the pit at some point farther down the path. It may help to know that you have plenty of company, but it helps even more to know how to join that remarkable breed of those who rise from the pit.

STEPS OUT OF THE PIT

The word *discouragement* has as its root the Latin word *cor,* which means "heart." As Dallas Willard reminds us in *Renovation of the Heart,* the Bible interchangeably uses the words *heart, will* or *spirit* not to describe the beating muscle in a person's chest but the "executive center" of the self. Your "heart" is the orienting, motivating, dynamic core of who you are. For this reason, God's Word says, "Above all else, guard your heart, / for it is the wellspring of life" (Proverbs 4:23).

To become *dis*-couraged, then, literally

> "CIRCUMSTANCES MAY APPEAR TO WRECK OUR LIVES AND GOD'S PLANS, BUT GOD IS NOT HELPLESS AMONG THE RUINS. OUR BROKEN LIVES ARE NOT LOST OR USELESS. GOD'S LOVE IS STILL WORKING. HE COMES IN AND TAKES THE CALAMITY AND USES IT VICTORIOUSLY, WORKING OUT HIS WONDERFUL PLAN OF LOVE."
>
> Eric Liddell, *Disciplines of the Christian Life*

means "to lose one's heart." It is to be separated from that strength of will, that driving spirit which enables someone to purpose mightily or act creatively. A discouraged person is spiritually "weary" to the point that he or she no longer feels the capacity for "doing good" (Galatians 6:9). Recovering one's heart (courage) is challenging because it requires taking active steps, and it is precisely the activating will or spirit that is damaged when discouragement sets in. Nonetheless, few leaders are ever robbed of their entire heart. Even the most discouraged among us has a heart that beats—however slowly, however dimly—and with God's grace it can rise again.

Should you, or someone under your leadership, ever find yourself in that deep and dark place, here are some specific steps worth taking.

Dare to cry for help. The first step toward recovery is to admit the reality of where we are and that we feel powerless. Sometimes, the dirt of discouragement pounds down so thickly on us that we truly cannot overcome its weight by ourselves. We need God, close friends, a pastor, counselor or—in some cases of severe depression or anxiety—a medical professional to help us get out of the pit. How many people remain stuck where they are simply because they lack the humility to cry for help?

Make real community a commitment. At the lowest point of his life as a leader, Elijah said, "I have been very zealous for the LORD God Almighty. The Israelites have rejected your covenant, broken down your altars, and put your prophets to death with the sword. I am the only one left" (1 Kings 19:10). God's response to Elijah is very instructive. He restored a framework of community for this lonely leader. First, God showed himself to Elijah to remind Elijah that he was not really alone. Second, he made Elijah aware of seven thousand others still devoted to the cause of God. And finally, God called Elijah to tap a successor.

Elijah's story has important lessons for all leaders. It's harder to fall into the well of discouragement and easier to get out again if you do, when you remain in vital relationship with God; with an intimate circle of peers who serve as mentors, companions and encouragers; and with some successors you are nurturing. Conversely, it is impossible to remain wholehearted as a leader without community. Discouragement feeds on isolation. Jesus faced his greatest temptations when he was alone in the wilderness. This is why he sent his disciples out two-by-two. It's also part of the reason he formed a church radically devoted to practicing the "one anothers" outlined in Scripture.[3]

So who are you close to in everyday *life?* Who are the people in your *leadership* team? Can you name those who will succeed you in building a *legacy?* Your answers make a profound difference in how you and others will deal with discouragement.

Resolve to be a great, old leader. When I (Dan) was in my twenties, I confided to a very seasoned leader how discouraged I felt when I compared my effectiveness to other leaders I saw. The older leader replied: "You have the wrong ambition. You want to be a perfect *performer* now, when the task of the moment is to be a terrific *learner.* Accept the fact that you'll need to make and learn from hundreds of mistakes to gain maturity. Resolve to be a great, *old* leader one day. Simply be "on the Way" now and you'll be amazed at what God does with that spirit." Jesus put it like this to his leading disciples: "Take my yoke upon you and learn from me, for I am gentle and humble in heart, and you will find rest for your souls. For my yoke is easy and my burden is light" (Matthew 11:29-30).

Is it possible that you have "heavier" standards for yourself than Jesus would lay on you? Are you willing to be patient with the time it takes to grow as a truly great leader? Archibald Hart, a mature mentor to thousands, writes that cultivating self-acceptance is absolutely crucial to the health of a Christian leader's heart. Amy Carmichael confesses:

> Sometimes when I read the words of those who have been more than conquerors, I feel despondent. I feel that I shall never be like that. But then I realize that they won step by step: by little bits of will; little denials of self; little inward victories; by faithfulness in very little things. They became what they are. No one sees these little hidden steps. They only see the accomplishment, but even so those small steps were taken. There is no sudden triumph, no sudden maturity. That is the work of the moment.[4]

Even the donkey understood the importance of those little steps.

Be careful as you count. As leaders, we will appropriately do some counting. Pastors tend to count the ABCs of attendance, buildings and contributions. Leaders of other kinds tend to count the DEFGs of dollars in, expenses out, future prospects and growth trends. Paying attention to metrics like these is surely part of the good stewardship a Christian leader must exercise. The Bible devotes plenty of text to numbering cubits, shekels and sheep. But a close study of the Scriptures makes it clear how much value God places on the HISs—hearts changed, intimacy (with him) gained, and service given. Putting numbers on these effects of a leader's ministry is much harder to do.

What is happening with the A-Gs may suggest these effects, but it is equally possible for a leader to be deceived by them. There have been many leaders who had large funds and followings who mattered little to the progress of the kingdom or who actually, perhaps unconsciously, labored against it. Think on this: At the most decisive and ultimately influential point of Christ's ministry as a leader—his work on the cross—his followers were dwindling, his bodily temple was collapsing, and his material resources were gone.

Before you let yourself become too crushed by the dirt of discouragement, when disappointment, frustration or failure feel overly heavy and the weight of your apparent worthlessness and loneliness seem more than you can bear, remember the cross. Remember that only God holds a Kingdom Calculator in his hand. As the aphorism goes: "Not everything that counts can be counted, and not every-

> "THE ESSENTIAL THING 'IN HEAVEN AND IN EARTH' IS . . . THAT THERE SHOULD BE LONG OBEDIENCE IN THE SAME DIRECTION, THERE THEREBY RESULTS, AND HAS ALWAYS RESULTED IN . . . SOMETHING WHICH HAS MADE LIFE WORTH LIVING."
>
> Friedrich Nietzsche, *Beyond Good and Evil*

thing that can be counted counts." The A-Gs are one set of indicators, but God urges us to see that they are not the only ones that matter in the metrics of HIS eternity.

Make faithfulness your highest goal. In his book *Holy Sweat,* Tim Hansel vividly recounts the story of Clarence Jordan, a man of remarkable ability—with doctorates in both agriculture and biblical languages—and the potential to do almost anything he wanted with his life. Clarence Jordan chose to serve the poor. During the 1940s he founded a farm in Americus, Georgia, that became a haven of hope for poor whites and blacks struggling to survive in the wake of the Great Depression.

As you can imagine, an institution like Jordan's Koinonia Farm didn't go over very big in the racially divided Deep South of the 1940s. Over the course of fourteen years the folks in his neighborhood showed just how much they liked Jordan's vision—boycotting him, slashing farm members' tires, and threatening worse. Finally, in 1954 the Ku Klux Klan decided they'd had enough of Clarence Jordan and determined to get rid of him once and for all. In the middle of the night they came hooded to the farm, set ablaze every one of its buildings, riddled Jordan's home with bullets and chased off every Koinonia family, save one.

The next day, a newspaper reporter came out to see what remained of the Koinonia Farm. Walking through smoldering rubble and scorched land, he found Jordan in the field—hoeing and planting. "I heard the *awful* news and I came out to do a story on the tragedy of your farm *closing*." Recognizing the voice of the reporter as belonging to one of the hooded figures who'd been there the night before, Clarence just kept on hoeing and planting. Determined to get the best of this man who ought to be packing his bags, the Klan member blurted, "Well, Dr. Jordan, you got two of them Ph.D.s and you've put fourteen years into this Farm, and there's nothing left of it all. Tell me, Doc, just how *successful* do you think you've been in the end?" Finally, Clarence stopped hoeing. Straightening his back, he turned toward the reporter, and with a gaze that could've melted ice, he said quietly but firmly, "I think we've been about as successful as the *Cross,* sir. You see, I don't think you really understand us. What we are about around here is not success; it's *faithfulness.*" And Clarence returned to his work.[5]

> "THERE IS NO DESPAIR SO ABSOLUTE AS THAT WHICH COMES WITH THE FIRST MOMENTS OF OUR FIRST GREAT SORROW, WHEN WE HAVE NOT YET KNOWN WHAT IT IS TO HAVE SUFFERED AND BE HEALED, TO HAVE DESPAIRED AND RECOVERED HOPE."
>
> George Eliot, *Adam Bede*

It is something to consider the HIS that has been the fruit of that faithfulness. Leaders like Jimmy Carter have had their vision stoked by it. Organizations like Habitat for Humanity have had their mission catalyzed by it. Countless individuals and families have seen their lives renewed by it. And all of this flowed from the heart of a Christian leader who refused to give up "doing good" when the current results were not what was hoped for.

The Living Bible translation of Galatians 6:9 reads: "Let us not get tired of doing what is right, for after awhile we will reap a harvest of blessings if we don't get discouraged and give up." Christian leaders are not machine workers but kingdom farmers. They know that faithfulness leads to fruitfulness and practice leads to produce, but that God alone is Lord of the harvest's timing, nature and magnitude.

For this reason faithful leaders practice a lifestyle of long-term *obedience* over short-term *expedience.* They keep shaking off the dirt that rains by the shovel loads upon them, resetting their feet and stepping up faithfully once more. And in this way they become among those who rise.

Remember whose kingdom prevails. This is the spirit we meet in the apostle Paul when he writes his last letter to Timothy from the dark, dank hole of the Mamertine Prison in Rome—actually a converted cistern—a well. From that place, Paul would certainly have been able to hear the sounds of laughter and commerce coming from the sunlight of the Roman Forum just above him—all the echoes of the earthly kingdom he had forsaken and which, in a very short while, would forsake him completely when Emperor Nero would order him beheaded, Peter crucified, and both of them buried.

We know from the things Paul says in 2 Timothy 4:9-16 that he is feeling the weight of death pressing on him. But then we hear the resilient beat of a heart which, though admittedly weary, refuses to give up. We feel the shudder of those shoulders muscled from the leadership trials of so many years. We watch as one more time Paul shakes the dirt of discouragement from his back, resets his feet and steps up faithfully. Gazing back across the long journey, Paul offers this final tribute to the Leader he has followed: "The Lord stood at my side and gave me strength, so that through me the message might be fully proclaimed and all the Gentiles might hear it. And I was delivered from the lion's mouth. The Lord will rescue me from every evil attack and will bring me safely to his heavenly kingdom. To him be glory for ever and ever. Amen" (2 Timothy 4:17-18).

Today, the Mamertine well is empty, a bit like a certain garden tomb outside Jerusalem. The Roman Forum lies in ruins, and people name their dogs after the emperor who once presided over it. But nearby, millions throng to glorious cathedrals named, like some of their children, after Paul and Peter. Millions more the world over humbly bend their knees in worship and service to the Lord for whom those leading disciples willingly gave their lives, because this Leader gave his life first for them. Colleges and universities; hospitals and orphanages; massive libraries and humanitarian agencies; entire systems of law, justice and economics; innumerable human stories—all stand as luminous witnesses to a Lord and kingdom no amount of dirt or death could finally bury.

So who is the bigger "donkey": a leader like Nero or one like Paul? Jesus never said that the journey of leadership would not involve some trials. Quite the contrary (see John 16:33). But he told us that he would be with us always (Matthew 28:20). He promised that he would provide the power needed to fulfill our mission (Acts 1:8). He guaranteed us that every investment we made in his kingdom would certainly last and pay off (Matthew 19:29; John 15:16). And Jesus assured us that if we kept placing our faith in him, one step at a time, there would be nothing that could finally bury us. We would be among those who rise (John 11:25).

> Therefore, . . . let us throw off everything that hinders and the sin that so easily entangles, and let us run with perseverance the race marked out for us. Let us fix our eyes on Jesus, the author and perfecter of our faith, who for the joy set before him endured the cross, scorning its shame, and sat down at the right hand of the throne of God. (Hebrews 12:1-2)

This is the high and humble call Christ issues to his leading disciples. And this call, Christ himself has issued to you.

---

[1]Eddie Gibbs, *LeadershipNext* (Downers Grove, Ill.: InterVarsity Press, 2005), p. 185.

[2]Archibald D. Hart, *Dark Clouds, Silver Linings* (Colorado Springs: Focus on the Family Publishing, 1993), p. 6.

[3]Love one another: Jn 13:34-35; Rom 12:10; 13:8; 1 Pet 1:22; 4:8. Pray for one another: 2 Thess 1:11; 3:1; Jas 5:16. Care for and comfort one another: 1 Cor 12:24-25; 1 Thess 4:18. Encourage and build up one another: 1 Thess 5:11; Heb 3:13; Jas 4:11; 5:9. Bear with and forgive one another: Rom 14:13; 15:7; Eph 4:2, 32; Col 3:13. Bear the burdens of one another: Gal 6:2. Admonish and instruct one another: Rom 15:14; Col 3:16. Spur one another on toward love and good deeds: Heb 10:24. Fellowship with one another: Acts 2:42-46; Heb 10:25; 1 Jn 1:7; Submit to and serve one another: Gal 5:13; Eph 5:21; 1 Pet 5:5; Extend hospitality to one another: 1 Cor 16:20; 2 Cor 13:12; 1 Pet 4:9; 5:14. Unite with one another: Rom 12:16; 1 Cor 1:10; 1 Pet 3:8.

[4]Amy Carmichael, quoted in Tim Hansel, *Holy Sweat* (Dallas: Word Publishing, 1987), p. 130.

[5]Hansel, *Holy Sweat,* pp. 188-89.

Leadership Exercise: Stepping Up, Out and On Your Way

1. As you sift through your own experience with the dirt of discouragement, which of the following have been particularly crushing or difficult for you?

    ____ disappointment ("It didn't happen like I'd hoped")
    ____ frustration ("God or other people failed me")
    ____ failure ("I blew it myself")
    ____ worthlessness ("I was not valued")
    ____ loneliness ("I felt very alone")

    What makes this so hard?

2. Which of the following signs of discouragement might someone have noticed if they got close enough to you?

    ____ anger   ____ depression   ____ resignation

    How does this show itself?

3. As you think about some of the suggested steps out of the pit of discouragement . . .
    • List some of the people who would likely respond helpfully if you cried out to them.
    •
    •
    •
    •
    •

- List the particular persons who make up the community to which you are regularly committed.

  mentors:

  peers:

  successors:

4. How do you respond to the idea of being content with becoming a great, *old* leader?

5. What specific qualities do you hope will have increased in you by the time your leadership journey is done?

6. What are you trying to count or discern as a measure of the effectiveness of your leadership?

7. What three things do you need to be especially faithful in sowing or being obedient to as you go forward in leadership?

   -

   -

   -

8. How are you encouraged by the truth that Christ's kingdom and way of leadership prevails?

Going Deeper

Farrar, Steve. *Finishing Strong: Going the Distance for Your Family.* Sisters, Ore.: Multnomah, 2000.

MacDonald, Gordon. *Restoring Your Spiritual Passion.* Nashville: Thomas Nelson, 1986.

Peterson, Eugene. *A Long Obedience in the Same Direction.* Downers Grove, Ill.: InterVarsity Press, 1980.

Yancey, Philip. *Disappointment with God.* Grand Rapids: Zondervan, 1992.

———. *Soul Survivor.* London: Hodder & Stoughton Religious, 2003.

ALSO AVAILABLE

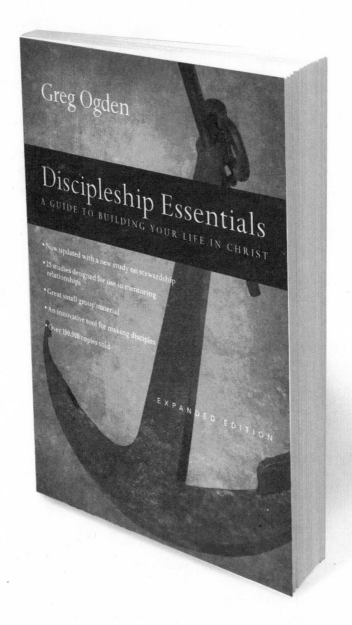

978-0-8308-1087-1, paper, 237 pages